THE RELEVANCE OF
CANADIAN HISTORY

THE RELEVANCE OF CANADIAN HISTORY:
U.S. and Imperial Perspectives

The 1977 Joanne Goodman Lectures
Delivered at the University of Western Ontario

By ROBIN W. WINKS
Professor of History
Master of Berkeley College
Yale University

Macmillan of Canada

Canadian Cataloguing in Publication Data

Winks, Robin W., 1930–
    The relevance of Canadian history

(The Joanne Goodman lectures; 1977)

ISBN 0-7705-1788-9

1. Canada – History – Addresses, essays, lectures.
I. Title. II. Series.

FC164.W55   971   C79-094133-3
F1026.W55

Printed in Canada for
The Macmillan Company of Canada Limited
70 Bond Street
Toronto, Ontario
M5B 1X3

CONTENTS

To James G. Allen, Charles S. Campbell,
Jr., and the Prince of Wales Hotel
Who and which started it all

FOREWORD

THE UNIVERSITY OF WESTERN ONTARIO WAS FORTUNATE TO have as its second Joanne Goodman Lecturer Professor Robin Winks of Yale University. In the first lectures Colonel Charles Stacey established the theme and tone of the series as he examined, in his delightful and inimitable manner, Canada's relations with the other two countries of the Atlantic Triangle in the first half of the twentieth century through the perceptions and policies of that uniquely tenacious and psychologically fascinating Prime Minister, Mackenzie King.

In the second series Robin Winks ranged even further to challenge his audience to consider the continuing interdependent relevance of Canadian, U.S., and British imperial history. For two days the university seemed truly a miniature universe as he plucked examples to illustrate his theme from his awesome store of knowledge of almost every country that was ever part of the British empire. The elegant and lucid lectures, delivered to a large audience of students, faculty, and the public, were all the more impressive for being given from a few notes. The published text, although different from the oral lectures and in another medium, accurately conveys the style of the spoken word. The first two lectures are a good guide to Professor Winks's reflections over the past two decades on Canadian history in relation to the history of the United States and the British Empire and Commonwealth; the third, the most global of all, is a tantalizing preview of his current research on American imperialism, in which his study of Canadian history will assuredly play an important part. Through the generosity of the lecture trust, this volume will allow the stimulating discussion begun by Professor Winks at Western to be continued in the international community of learning.

It is a common complaint of Canadians that no one outside the country is interested in our history. This certainly cannot be said of Robin Winks. His energy and curiosity have carried him around the globe and into the history of many countries. But although he is committed to the comparative study of problems rather than the history of single countries, he has published important works on purely Canadian topics, most notably *Canada and the United States: The Civil War Years* (1960) and *The Blacks in Canada* (1971). These books have been enriched by his international perspective as they in turn have contributed to his comparative studies. In addition to being a member of the Yale history department since 1957, Professor Winks is also advisor to the library on Commonwealth history and literature, and, since these lectures were delivered, Master of Berkeley College. From 1969 to 1971 he served as Cultural Attaché in the American embassy in London. He has lectured at universities around the world, including many in Canada, for which he is almost a permanent cultural attaché at large.

The Joanne Goodman Lectures were established in 1975 as a living memorial to the elder daughter of Mr. and Mrs. Edwin A. Goodman of Toronto. Each year a distinguished scholar is invited to the University of Western Ontario to deliver three public lectures on some aspect of the history of the English-speaking peoples, particularly the Atlantic Triangle of Canada, the United Kingdom, and the United States. The lectures already play an important part in the intellectual life of the university and in their published form will provide a major contribution to historical literature. The University of Western Ontario is grateful to Mr. and Mrs. Goodman and their family and friends for this generous and moving benefaction dedicated to a student who loved history and enjoyed her years at this university.

Neville Thompson
The University of Western Ontario
September 1978

PREFACE

WHEN THE UNIVERSITY OF WESTERN ONTARIO ASKED ME TO give the Joanne Goodman Lectures in January of 1977, I felt a special sense of delight not alone because it is a distinct honour for me, as a citizen of the United States, to be asked to speak on Canadian history to a Canadian audience. Twenty-three years ago, I visited the University of Western Ontario as an American graduate student working on a doctoral dissertation on Canadian-American relations during the American Civil War, and I received the warmest possible welcome from Fred Landon, a scholar beloved to the University, to London, and to Canadianists everywhere. My pleasure was further increased when I learned that the first annual Goodman Lectures had been delivered in March 1976 by that redoubtable warrior of Canadian historiography, Colonel Charles P. Stacey, for he, too, in his gruff and ever helpful way, had guided me through the thickets of Canadian research on that first foray into unknown territory. To have Colonel Stacey present for the second lecture, joined by Mr. and Mrs. Edwin Goodman and their daughter Diane throughout the lectures, more than offset the cold Canadian welcome outside the lecture hall.

I gave much thought at the time to the question of why I, as an American teaching (at least to a substantial extent) Canadian history in an American university, should have been invited as the second Goodman lecturer. I was mindful, of course, of the fact that the lectures were intended to explore the history of the English-speaking peoples, and particularly the nations that formed the North Atlantic Triangle of J. Bartlet Brebner's title. Most Canadians (and most Americans) assume that I am Canadian — an interesting example of Canadians' tendency to underrate themselves, for who else, they appear to reason, would be interested in Canadian history other than a fellow, if transplanted, Canadian? What an unusual thought, that someone born in Indiana and growing up in Colorado should care about Canadian history! As I reflected upon this common misapprehension about the place an interest in Canada takes in the popular conception of History broadly viewed, I decided that the theme of my lectures should demonstrate why I believe Canadian history seems so important, not to Canadians, but to Americans, Nigerians, and scholars of modern Britain. I also wanted to demonstrate that, to me at least, Canadian history is very exciting.

In the United States one can with little effort make Canadian history relevant to a variety of historical questions usually thought to be largely non-Canadian in origin or content. My argument in part, I thought, might please Canadian nationalists: Canadian history is important. I also found that it displeased other Canadian nationalists, for, as will be seen, in giving the lectures I maintained that Americans should study Canada for American not Canadian reasons. This is not to say that Canadian history is not worthy of study for its own sake, just as Bach is alleged to have defended his music on the grounds that "it was for the greater glory of God — and because he enjoyed it". None the less, I also maintained that the citizens of any nation study the history and culture of another nation for reasons arising from their own needs. Put differently, Canadians study the history of the United States for different reasons — and thus differently — than do Americans, or Germans, or Iranians. I thought and still think it quite reasonable to assume that Americans would study Canadian history only if its relevance could clearly be demonstrated to them.

But I come to Canadian history (or Australian, or Malaysian history, for that matter) with another conviction in mind. For a long time, I think, most universities in much of the world have made a mistake in organizing their history curricula around national identities. Look at almost any university catalogue, including that of my own university; you will find it replete with courses called The History of France, The History of Great Britain, The History of Germany, The History of the United States: 1492 to 1865, The History of the United States: 1865 to the Present, The History of Canada. What such organization almost invariably does, certainly for the less perceptive student, is induce a subtle Whig bias by which students are led to the conclusion that what history is all about is the rise of the nation state, and that one is studying history as a discipline primarily to learn why and how this nation or that nation came to be as it was and as it is. This conclusion in turn leads research students to the conclusion that the nation state is the best receptacle for the collection of historical data.

Stated in these terms, the contention is obviously false. The best receptacle for the collection of historical data clearly is not the nation state. Lord Acton was right when he enjoined us to study problems. If a problem is taken as the unit of study, however — that is, if one studies revolutions, not a revolution, studies imperialisms, not the imperialism of a single nation, studies bi-culturalism, not one nation state's bi-culturalism — then one is engaging by the nature of things in comparative history. This has the disadvantage of appearing to be merely fashionable to some. It has the very real disadvantage of being very difficult, requiring that the scholar break from the mould of single-language training and single-culture interpretations. It has the enormous disadvantage, in a world of those who perish if they do not publish, of being time-consuming and open to many potential dead ends.

Even so, and acknowledging the risks of superficiality, I have concluded that the historian of the United States who is ignorant of Canadian history is ignorant of his own history. (The converse is also true.) I maintain that any Africanist who does not know some Canadian history is an ignorant Africanist, given the impact of Canadian events on the ultimate mode of decolonization chosen by the United Kingdom. Any person who knows only Louis Riel and not Wavoka, who knows only the Ghost Dance and not the Hau-Hau of New Zealand, who knows only Maji Maji and not Riel, who cannot view all these forms of effort at indigenous revitalization as variants on a common theme in the history of Western imperialism is the poorer for that.

In short, the reason Americans should study Canadian history is to learn more about themselves, about how they differ from and how they are similar to others. Once this motivation to study Canadian history is clearly understood, I find that Americans are happy to study Canadian history, for naturally they wish to learn more about themselves. One then engages in that nice activity in which so many Canadians engaged in the 1920s, bootlegging, bringing information about Canada into a course which students perceive to be largely about their own world environment. Somewhere near the end of such a course, students often discover that they know quite a bit about Canada too.

These, then, were the arguments I rehearsed to myself as I prepared the lectures that follow, and this, then, explains why the content of the lectures so often wanders away from Canada *per se*. Having confessed this, two other confessions remain to be made. The lectures were not read; they were spoken from notes. This may have led me into egregious error; it certainly gave the lectures the air of being rather like something out of Pirandello, not as Six Characters in Search of an Author but as random notes in search of a speech. Moreover, events arose between the giving and the revising of the lectures for publication — events in Quebec which should be reflected in the revisions and are not, events in my own life which help account for but do not justify the delay in publication. For this delay I am solely responsible, for the publisher, my hosts, and my sponsor waited patiently. As a result, the lectures are in no sense an exact record of what I said on those cold, yet warm, days in January 1977 when I had the honour to deliver these words in memory of Joanne Goodman, a second-year history student at the University of Western Ontario who died in a highway accident in April 1975.

Robin W. Winks
Berkeley College
Yale University

PART I ♘ CANADIAN HISTORY AND THE CASE FOR COMPARATIVE STUDIES

THOSE WHO FEEL NERVOUS OF COMPARATIVE HISTORY INVARI-
ably raise certain objections. There is the objection that the
comparative approach is, in a variety of ways, restricted
because it looks only at those problems capable of comparison. Surely this is true. That is to say, it is a mistake to
compare the British Empire with the Roman Empire, a
favourite game of the British themselves at the end of the
nineteenth and in the early part of the twentieth century,
a game by which they could congratulate themselves and
make foolish predictions about the length of time for which
the British Empire would continue to thrive. In fact this is
an illegitimate comparison, then and now, because the
technologies in which the two empires grew were so utterly
different as to defy any legitimacy in comparing the realities of the impact of their cultures upon other, less complex,
technologies. One must begin, to be sure, with elements,
societies, problems which are in truth comparable.

Second, it is often argued that one cannot engage in
comparative studies because inevitably what one does will
be superficial. This is true as well, yet inevitably what one
does in national history is also superficial, and in more
subtle and socially dangerous ways. Third, many comparative historians are in fact not doing comparative history,
whatever they may say. They are engaging in what might
best be called parallel studies or the study of the impact of
one society upon another.[1]

Some fifteen years ago, when, by the nature of events, I
was much younger, I attempted to launch a series of vol-
umes (not one of which ever appeared) to be published by

the Yale and the McGill university presses jointly, which were meant to be on the Canadian-American experience comparatively viewed. Not having done enough thinking about the problem, I designed a number of subjects about, for example, the assumed impact of Massachusetts and New York school laws on Ontario education, or the ways in which the labour movement in both countries interacted. I am delighted today that none of those books was ever written, at least to my specifications, because they would have been on the wrong track. The study of the impact of one society upon another is not comparative studies, it is a particular type of the study of intellectual, or social, or even of diplomatic history.

What comparative history does do, it seems to me, is help us to escape from the assumption that a particular course of events is natural, almost foreordained. Until, for example, historians began to study societies in which there were substantial black or minority populations, and in which there was no legal segregation, how were they to know that the experience in the American South was not "natural", even though generations of historians — most obviously U. B. Phillips — wrote of that experience as though it were natural. One unhappy effect of assuming that any historical experience is natural is the further assumption that very little can be done about events, that what is was meant to be, the natural unfolding of "the course of history", whatever that may mean. Only after scholars began to look to other frontiers than the American — for example to the Australian, the South African, or the Canadian — did they begin to recognize that the violence that occurred on the American frontier was unusual, since other frontiers did not experience this kind of violence. Only thus did American historians begin to ask questions about why, then, was there segregation in the South? Why, then, was there a turn to vigilante justice in the American West? Until American scholars had asked parallel questions about other societies, they could not frame comparative questions about their own society correctly. Thus it seems to me that comparative studies, above all, helps one overcome the "natural", conservative bias that history is simply one damn thing after another and helps one begin to associate some sophisticated causal patterns with the continuum from past to present.

I wish to explore three case studies in the comparative method by way of examples. Let us begin with that cliché of Americans who view Canada: that Canadians are basically like Americans, except that it is colder and snows more often in Canada and that Canadians have a monarchical and parliamentary system of government. At bed rock, Americans think, the Canadian experience is not all that different from the experience of the United States. I believe this to be a false conception, and I would like to engage in a series of broad generalities meant to demonstrate why it is a false statement. I look first to American history.

American historians over the last several generations have attempted to interpret the warp and the woof of the American experience in a variety of ways. I think it fair to conclude that three major interpretations have come to be widely accepted, vulgarized, and placed into American collegiate and secondary-school textbooks, so that most educated or even quasi-educated Americans have come to share the assumptions inherent in these three interpretations. Let me rehearse, briefly, those interpretations which have so dominated American self-perception.

The first interpretation is associated with a name already a cliché in Canadian history as well, Frederick Jackson Turner.[2] Turner's thesis, delivered in an address in Chicago in 1893, rested upon his conclusion that the American frontier had closed, this assumption itself arising from a particular definition that he chose to apply to the frontier. With the closing of the frontier, he thought, those motive forces which had made Americans what they had been in the past would in all probability cease to exist in the future, and Americans would become a different people in the twentieth century. He argued that Americans became a different people — that is, different from Europeans — by virtue of the existence of free land on a moving frontier. (Although the frontier was progressing westwards, there were exceptions, as in the movement into Maine, or the rapid leap across the great basin and plains region to California, which made the frontier movement become in fact an eastern movement back into the empty area.) He held that in the process of movement across the land those who came to the new world set down their old cultural baggage, or cultural traits, and out of their confrontation with the new environment began to manufacture for themselves and from their experience new cultural baggage.

There is at first glance nothing unusual about this argument. Any immigrant community has undergone a process of adaptation anywhere in the world. What was unusual, Turner thought, was that the process took place time and time again, over a short span of time, so that the American people experienced these adaptations to new environments with greater rapidity across a wider variety of landscapes and under the impact of a more rapidly changing technology than any other people in the history of the world. Two corollaries of the Turner thesis, therefore, were that the greater the westward movement the more democratic (or unEuropean) the American people would become; thus the quintessential American was someone from the West. Further, this process would need to be continued by artificial means, if necessary, if the American were to retain his sense of identity and those qualities that made him so distinct from the European; Turner described the American as aggressive, materialistic, philanthropic, optimistic. He designed an image not unlike that of a moving glacier, in which he saw small pockets of the previous cultural norm being retained, not wiped out, as the glacial movement took place across the frontier line. One could expect to find in, say, Tennessee, or in southern Indiana, cultures that were not changing with the same rapidity as the national norm. Broadly viewed, such pockets might have so much in common as to constitute a coherent section, a substantially different culture within the national fabric. Such sectionalism would lead, of course, to tension within American society and to a wide diversity of definitions of what America's goals should be. He therefore added, in a separate essay on the significance of sections on American history, that the states were depositories of assumptions about the nature of the law in American society. They provided the real focus for American loyalties, for the American first identified himself with his state before he identified himself with his nation. Because of the federal structure of the American government, much of the law that would actually pervade the life of the individual would be local law; in this way the sense of locality would be preserved. It was state laws that would define at what age one might marry, under what conditions one might divorce, at what age one might take a drink (and whether it would be beer or wine, and whether one could take that drink standing up or sitting down, in the presence of someone of the opposite sex or never in the presence of someone of the opposite sex). It would be a state law that would define most crimes and the punishment for most crimes. It would be state laws that would most circumscribe the daily activities of the individual, not federal laws, and thus there would continue to be wide diversities on a regional basis.

The second of the great theses that have clearly crept into the textbooks is one associated with David M. Potter and best expressed in his book, *People of Plenty*, which consists of a series of lectures delivered in Chicago, in 1950.[3] Potter's thesis (I now oversimplify badly) was that Turner was correct in looking to the land, that is to say, to the environment, as the principal determining factor in the emergence of an American identity and in the ability of Americans to divest themselves of their European characteristics, but that Turner had failed to see the primary significance of the land. That primary significance arose from the concept of abundance: there was always enough, there was indeed always more than enough, so that the American was optimistic, materialistic, yet also philanthropic and aggressive, because there was more to be had, more natural resources, more land, more population streaming in from the great immigration sources. The American saw the West as the land of beginning again, saw the experience of mobility as the chief indicator of *being* an American, and thus that experience consisted not in putting roots down in a single place but in carrying one's roots with one's self.

Let us look at Turner and Potter together for a moment.[4] America did not develop a landed aristocracy, because there was so much land and because it was spread so broadly in terms of a thin population that virtually anyone who wished to possess realty could do so. Furthermore, movement across this land would take place in such a way and with so many opportunities open to those who would move across it that no employer could squeeze his employees unduly. Rather than strike against him they could simply close up their shop and move westward. Nor could employees demand too much of the employer, or he too could close his shop and move westward, leaving them without employment. This kind of amelioration of European class conflict did seem to occur in the sense that employer and employee did not come to the clash that nineteenth-century Marxist theory suggested that they must. One could close a textile mill on the Thames River, in Connecticut, and move elsewhere in Connecticut, leaving one's employees without work. Or the employees could move from the textile mill to a brass factory in Danbury. (In reality movement did occur, although not to the West so much as within the East.)

As Americans moved across the continent, they left behind them, then, that series of cultural deposits. Each deposit increasingly was removed from European cultural norms, and while the east coast of America remained more nearly a fragment of European society, by the time one had moved through a great variety of other environments one had produced a truly unique civilization. The "real" American would be found, then, both in a place — the West — and at the end of a process. This glacial theory of terminal and lateral moraines is really an Hegelian dialectic. Indeed it is Marxist in its approach, and it is said by some that Turnerians are Marxists in disguise, although most Turnerians would not care to admit it. It is materialistic, emphasizing an economic determination which dwells upon land — upon size, upon space, and upon its relative value in terms of the population. The Marxist connotations of Turner were readily ignored, however, as were his pessimistic implications: that when the free land was gone, American institutions might cease to be democratic. The optimistic Turner was taken up by the American people: Americans were different, they could continue to be different, and they would continue to move on the roads of progress because of the very processes that arose from the uniqueness of their environment.

Potter, then, taking the notion of abundance, argued that Americans had become what Turner said they had become because there was always More: more of everything. There was more land when it was needed; there were more resources; there was more space; there were more people. It was, in large measure, because of its economic abundance that America became a unique and democratic nation. What Potter appeared to be saying was that Americans became a democracy because they were rich enough to do so; he went on explicitly elsewhere to argue that Americans should not expect poor nations to become democracies, since democracy rests upon affluence.

Potter was not trying to destroy the Turnerian view, for

he agreed that the frontier experience was basic to the American character. One reason Potter thought it necessary to say this arises from the second level of the largely mythical theory to which I am referring — the way in which government officials from time to time have used the notion of the Frontier in American history. Increasingly, politicians have felt it necessary to "get right" with the Frontier. American politicians had always found it necessary to "get right with Lincoln", as the phrase had it; increasingly, they wanted to get right with the West as well — not the West as a place, but the West as a process. In 1932, Franklin Delano Roosevelt, in an address before the Commonwealth Club (before he was in office), declared that the problems of America stemmed from the fact that the Frontier had closed, and that his New Deal would create a new frontier by which the small businessman, the true individualist in a capitalist society, once again would be able to grow. This is not to say that Roosevelt had read his Turner; he probably had not; but someone — Rexford Guy Tugwell, perhaps? — had thrust some quotations from Turner before him, and he had absorbed them. He did see that Americans would respond to the challenge of "getting back" to the conditions that had made America great in the nineteenth century, to "getting back to the Frontier", the land of eternal return, the Fountain of Youth.

Another historian — the creator of my third thesis — who recognized that the Frontier was becoming a political myth rather than a regional reality was C. Vann Woodward. In 1961, also in Chicago, in an address which he called "The Age of Reinterpretation", Woodward argued that American society was changing and would change at a revolutionary pace in the future, and that it would be necessary to reinterpret American history in the light of those changes, since they would bring to the surface an awareness of events and movements that had not been properly analysed by historians in the past. One of the fundamental changes that he foresaw related to what has since been called his "free security thesis".[5] Woodward argued that the frontier, as distance and as space, shaped the American character with a security that was free. That is to say, free of charge: the American people had been secure from outside threat for a long period of time without having to spend any money to achieve that security, for during the nineteenth century, when European nations fought a succession of wars and spent a considerable proportion of their national incomes on the maintenance of navies, armies, colonial establishments, foreign offices, and universities that would teach tropical medicine, the United States had spent its money upon developing its frontier.

Whom, after all, had the United States to fear? Surely neither nation with which it shared its borders, for Canada was a dependency of a European power and a hostage to that power's good behaviour in the New World, while Mexico was a weak, once-defeated neighbour of no military significance. What jackboots need Americans fear, other than internal enemies? The United States had therefore overtaken Britain and Germany (the latter in the process of overtaking the former) at a phenomenal rate, and had become the leading industrial nation of the world before the end of the nineteenth century, all at relatively little cost to itself. The fact that Americans had never thought in terms of wars fought for limited objectives, of wars which could not become moral crusades, but always had thought of total wars, meant that Americans had not developed a sense of evil and of the need, on occasion, to live with it. The frontier had provided national (not local, to be sure) security; Americans developed an isolated, unique democracy which did not have to come to terms with a number of realities which would face the world once the frontier had disappeared.

Note that all three of these historians were agreed upon a single, fundamental point: that the Frontier had closed, and that the element that they preferred to emphasize in terms of the shaping of the American character was no longer operative. Turner said there no longer was a Frontier; Potter said there no longer was natural economic abundance: advertising, in order to create a continued, if artificial, economy of abundance, had arisen in America instead; Woodward said there no longer was free security. The myths upon which Americans had fed themselves from at least 1893 until the 1960s had been shown to be irrelevant to the future. One must anticipate, therefore, that the American character not only would be changing drastically, but that Americans themselves would enter a period of turbulent confusion as nostalgia battled with an unknown and feared future.

The Frontier, then, was not only a state of mind; it was a place, quite genuinely, and it was also a process, as Turner pointed out. Turner recognized, for that matter, that the Frontier was all three of these, shifting, metaphorically, from meaning to meaning. The West was "a land of beginning again", it was that which made possible the eternal genesis in the American character; it explained why Americans always seem to spring youthfully upon the world, full of energy, always hurrying, busy, busy, a kind of buckskin *beau sauvage* who were constantly moving westward until they ran into the true *beau sauvage*, when both discovered that one could also be *ignoble sauvage*.

Now each of these three theses utterly separates the experience of the United States from the experience of Canada. Examine these three theses — belief patterns which are the guiding principles of most Americans in their understanding of their history to the end of the 1960s, theses which encapsulate what Hans Kohn would have called "the vital lies" of American society.[6] (By "vital lies" Kohn meant "truths" that are accepted and incapable of disproof, which have such great vitality that, though they may be lies, they have the force of truth.) Not one of these three theses could possibly be written today by a Canadian scholar about the Canadian experience. (To be sure, Canadian scholars at one stage were sufficiently imitative of scholars from the United States that they wanted to borrow the Turner thesis, and several efforts were made to create a Turnerian-style analysis for the Canadian experience, especially for British Columbia.)[7]

Why not? In Canada there have been four distinct frontiers, as well as other minor examples of the phenomenon usually meant to be described by the word. There was a French frontier in the New World which lasted approximately from 1534 until 1760. There was an English frontier settlement associated primarily with Upper Canada (later to be called Canada West and later yet Ontario), an experience concentrated in the years between 1783 and 1837. There was the western frontier of open spaces, essentially unwooded, explored and developed between the 1840s and 1920. There was a frontier of the far North, known from the earliest days of European contact when Martin Frobisher first sought a Northwest Passage, and not fully exploited to this day. Physically and chronologically these frontiers paralleled developments in the United States. Because of superficial similarities, Canadian historians — beginning with Walter Sage, and, more cautiously, A. L. Burt and A. R. M. Lower — embraced the "frontier thesis", and until the late 1930s much of Canadian history was interpreted in the light of Turnerian analysis. Today, partly as a result of the rise of the Laurentian School of Canadian historians who emphasize east-west trading routes and the influence of the St. Lawrence River, partly because of the insights provided by comparative historians and sociologists, most scholars would agree that, while there were a series of Canadian frontiers, the total meaning of the frontier experience for Canada was quite different from that for the United States.

The French frontier in Canada was at the outer limit of continental European culture. Commerce expanded upon the basis of the frontier, creating an expansion of ideas. If the Renaissance freed the mind and Luther freed the spirit as preconditions to the new opportunities and enlarged economic horizons of which the very word "frontier" was a metaphor, a new environment was necessary in which these new freedoms might find expression. In general, they did so in North America, but far less so in French Canada, where the basic thrust was almost entirely commercial, where control was vested solely in a distant, politically conservative capital, and where there was little opportunity for religious, political, or commercial innovation. Walter Prescott Webb has argued that through exploiting the New World the stable European population was presented with a surplus of land and capital, launching four hundred years of boom. Yet, for the most part, the closed Colbertian world of New France did not significantly alter the land-people-capital ratio, and the French frontier in Canada was neither a primary source of boom for France nor itself a land of opportunity. The economic impact of America on Europe usually is summarized in terms of bullion, trade, and entrepreneurship — that is, in terms of mercantilism. Precisely because French mercantilism differed from British, so too did the French frontier differ from the British frontier.

New France experienced four types of frontier, but these types did not appear in successive waves, as Turner's typonomy suggested, for they were simultaneous, coterminous, and static. The commercial, religious, military, and settlement frontiers of New France were aspects of a single, obsessive concern for profit. Few settlers came to New France with the intention of remaining permanently. Relatively little economic opportunity was open to the residents, and what there was was fixed to staple dependency upon the fur trade and the success of the *coureurs de bois*. Religion was, if anything, more conservative, ultramontane, and erastian than in France itself. The French frontier was of the whole of New France, not just on the fringes of settlement, and it did not advance steadily westward or in any other direction, for movement was not its purpose. The French frontier was static, opposed to change, antithetical to the usual romantic meanings given to the word "frontier" itself. Only when the British acquired New France in the conquest of 1759 did the frontier of settlement move forward to overwhelm the frontier of stability.

The second, or British, frontier was best expressed in Upper Canada, but it was to be found in all areas of new settlement, especially after 1783, in the Maritime colonies or along the St. Lawrence and the Great Lakes. Upper Canada received a steady influx of settlers, "Late Loyalists", Quakers, Mennonites, Dunkards, blacks, land speculators, foresters, Americans, Irish, all mixed in the eastern townships of Lower Canada (later Canada East and now Quebec), or in Upper Canada from the Bay of Quinte to the Niagara River. Here the Canadian frontier was, for the first and also for the last time, similar to the American frontier. Upper Canadian farmers, in a wooded temperate zone, grew wheat, oats, and barley, produced whisky, sought improved transportation through canals and railroads, and were dependent on faraway markets. In common with most frontiers, Upper Canada lacked capital, and a few merchants took leading positions in shaping society. The settlers showed the usual concern for education, for imported high culture, for temperance societies, and for a rude equality in speech, manners, and dress. But there were differences between the Canadian and American frontiers which began to set them apart even so early as the 1830s.

Some of these differences were obvious at the time. Except for Spanish-speaking frontiersmen who seldom were settlers, the American frontier was ethnically one. There were minorities, to be sure, and many languages would be heard on the American frontier, especially in river towns such as St. Louis. But in Canada one-third of the population was French speaking: too large a minority to ignore, too small and isolated a culture to dominate. Further, its ratio to the total population remained relatively constant. For the most part, French Canadians stayed within their province, leaving the exploitation of the cheap lands of Upper Canada to the new arrivals, *revanches des berceaux* increasing their numbers in step with growth by immigration elsewhere. The majority of the new arrivals were Americans, and many were loud in their desire for annexation of this frontier which seemed physically so similar to Ohio or northeast Indiana. On the American frontier, each new arrival strengthened the security of the settlement against the chief source of fear, the Indian, so that growth meant greater national security; on the Upper Canadian frontier, new arrivals from America decreased security, for the Indian posed no threat while the potentially subversive American did. In the United States, in short, More meant Safer, while in Canada More meant Weaker. Finally, once Upper Canada had been developed, once the Rebellion of 1837 had been suppressed by the Crown, and once the Annexation Manifesto of 1849 had been proved hollow bombast, Canadians who chose to move westward would do so by moving into the United States. The Great Canadian Shield, on which agriculture was most difficult, swept down to touch Lake Superior at Thunder Bay, severing any possibility of a continuous line of agricultural settlements and diverting the Canadian westward movement to south of the Great Lakes. It is at this point that the Canadian frontier began to diverge most strikingly from the Turnerian model.

Attempts to apply Turner's thesis, or close variants of it, to the Canadian frontier have been mistaken, then; for that frontier has been markedly different from the frontier in the United States. There are three fundamental reasons why this is so. First, Canada remained a monarchy. Second, none of the criteria most commonly associated with the American frontier — "free land", "abundance", or "free security" — applied to Canada. Third, the Canadian frontier lacked the environmental diversity over which the process was played out in the United States, and its basic thrust was northward rather than westward.

That Canada remained a monarchy is of fundamental

importance if one accepts that frontiers create a selecting (or at least a filtering) process. Encounters with new environments in North America forced Europeans to reconsider the cultural baggage they had brought with them, ultimately to create new cultural baggage in response to new demands. But in Canada different selectors were at work, and different cultural baggage was involved from the outset. At the time of the American Revolution, the "Canadian frontier" lay all about one: in Nova Scotia, where Halifax had been founded as recently as 1749; in New Brunswick, then still part of Nova Scotia; and in Upper and Lower Canada. All four of these colonies received major injections of new settlers as a direct result of the Revolution, the eastern townships of Lower Canada and the Saint John River Valley of New Brunswick being settled almost wholly by Loyalists who had remained constant to the British Crown. Their attitudes, while innovative towards tools and physical artifacts, were bound to remain conservative in political and social expression, and to this day comparative sociologists would agree that Canadian customs are more conservative and at least marginally closer to European norms than those of the United States.

The monarchy continued to influence the cultural baggage, however. While French-speaking Canadians had no reason to love the British Crown, they feared it less — since the Crown had confirmed their religion, language, and law to them — than they feared the United States. As Lord Elgin, a Governor General, was to remark, the last hand to wave the British flag in Canada would be a French hand. Despite vast empty tracts of land stretching back from the St. Lawrence, most French Canadians lived in towns from the outset, and their culture, while often rural, seldom partook of the distances and the dangers of a genuine frontier. The British settlers, many of them demobilized soldiers given grants of land, or collective colonists sent from Scotland as a group, moved onto the land far more slowly than American settlers did, and were from the start under the control of the common law.

This difference is especially telling. Americans felt that they could shape their own laws to fit their new experiences. While the riparian codes or mining laws of the new western states were in part copied from the eastern states, they were organic to the extent that they were modified in important ways locally; and in any event their most immediate models were North American. Settlers often had established themselves before Congress had provided territorial government, so that in many local ways the settlers along the pushing edge of the American frontier could believe that they were shaping their own laws. Not so in Canada, where a myth of sociological jurisprudence could not take root. Long before Canadian settlers had pressed into the western lands, both the common law and the specific regulations of that powerful, semi-feudal, chartered company — the Hudson's Bay Company — had been placed upon the land. Settlers could conform or leave, but, with the exceptions of Vancouver Island and British Columbia before 1871, they were not free to shape laws in accordance with their own perceptions of their immediate environment. Thus Canadians showed different attitudes towards the law itself, towards the function of the state, towards education, and towards governance than Americans did, and while these differences were in many instances of degree rather than of kind, the degree was significant.

Because the land was Crown land, or Company land, it was not free in the moral, legal, or social sense. Because transportation was difficult, a trans-Canadian railroad not being completed until 1885 and a paved trans-Canadian highway not until the 1960s, movement westward beyond the fertile agricultural lands of Ontario was difficult. When that movement took place, it often was through the United States, where many settlers stopped without going further. During the decades between 1910 and 1930, when the Canadian West received its greatest proportionate population increase, land was cheap, but at the end of this period the crops best grown on that land, from which the United States had gained so much, were no longer in demand.

Abundance for Canada often meant staple production. While a succession of staples — codfish, furs, timber, wheat, and minerals — gave Canada a specific economic role to play, this role was hampered by three considerations, so that genuine abundance in the sense of an attitude of mind which always assumed that prosperity lay just around the corner seldom came to Canadians. The economic role of Canada was played primarily within the context of the British Empire (and, after 1931, the British Commonwealth) with the aid of Commonwealth preferences, while the American economic role was worldwide. The staples themselves, while abundant, often were brought onto the world market just as the item was entering a decline: the beaver pelts of Hudson Bay, the wheat of Saskatchewan, the aluminium of British Columbia. Further, Canada showed many of the characteristics of a staple-dependent economy, such as Cuba has been, while the products of the American frontier were far more varied, moved onto world markets at an earlier time, and also had a substantial domestic market upon which to feed.

The American West provided the United States with distance — with space as a protection against potential enemies. The Canadian West led not to "free security" but to a constant fear of annexation, for Canada was exposed the further west settlement moved from its essentially trans-Atlantic political, social, and economic ties. The Canadian West did not, therefore, become a symbol of the Canadian future, except during the short period of time preceding World War I when the Minister of Immigration asked for strong-armed yeomen in sheepskin jackets to people the plains. Many of these men in sheepskin jackets came from the adjacent American states, however, increasing the dangers of an American cultural, if not political, annexation, so that the cry of More Men still meant to many Canadians a greater danger of loss of a precious identity rather than, as in the American West, a reinforcement of an identity presumed to be unique.

That the Canadian frontier lay primarily to the north of a thin line of towns, strung out, to paraphrase Hugh MacLennan, like rosary beads, each a worry to London and to Ottawa, meant that the frontier was essentially a story of Northernism rather than of Westering. Environmental similarity marked the northern lands, and this similarity included the impracticality of large-scale settlement on semi-barren tundra, the inability to create chains of villages to sustain railroads built by private enterprise (hence the growth of a Canadian mixed-enterprise economy), and an awareness that the northern frontier would produce an extractive economy. Riches would flow into Bay Street or other financial centres and locally oriented subeconomies would develop more slowly than in the United States, where settlement in such climatically diverse environments as the Dakotas, New Mexico, and Florida (still a frontier land as a whole, demographically, until the 1920s) would lead to diversity.

For these reasons, then, the Canadian frontier differed from the American. The differences themselves could be seen in many ways. Canadians showed an attraction for group or collective heroes, since their environment was to be mastered more by organization men — the Hudson's Bay Company trapper, factor, or trader; the Royal Canadian Mounted Policeman; the Saskatchewan grain-growers' associations; or, earlier, the servants of New France — than by individuals. Since the Canadian frontier was not occupied by Indian tribes prepared to resist European encroachment, and since the French early had learned to use the woodlands Indians as allies, neither the British government nor the Canadian settlers turned to policies of genocide to clear the aboriginal population from the land. There were few colourful Indian wars and relatively little bloodshed, and, while the Indian was not well treated, he did survive near or even on his ancestral lands. Since there were no cattle kingdoms, no trail drives, and little vigilante justice, the most colourful episodes associated with the West of American myth-makers could not be transplanted to Canadian locales. The Canadian West did not experience all of Turner's successive waves of newcomers in the order he suggested. Since the Canadian frontier was not a turbulent one, direct governmental intervention was required only twice — in the two Métis rebellions of 1869 and 1884, both led by Louis Riel — and the horse, the gun, and the shoot-out at the o.k. Corral did not acquire the glamour given to them by the American frontier.

This being so, the Canadian frontier did not take root in the national literature in the same way that it did in American literature. To be sure, Canadian literature is marked by an awareness of environment, of landscape, waterscape, and cloud; yet this awareness draws as much upon the romanticism of Wordsworth and the Lake Poets as it does upon the frontier. The leading Canadian poets would sing of epic explorations, of the long contest between French and British, or of small urban triumphs and defeats, but seldom of the West as such. The Canadian West did produce a literature of agrarian defeat — of the loneliness expressed by Hamlin Garland — in such writers as Sinclair Ross, and it also produced a literature of spiritual uplift which suggested that frontiersmen and those close to the soil were closer to God (as Willa Cather did on occasion for Nebraska, and Ralph Connor — pseudonym for Charles W. Gordon — did for the sweep of land between Manitoba and Alberta), and in these ways the literatures of the frontiers were similar. Still there was a difference, for western-based Canadian literature was the story of the immigrant, of the new arrival: Canadian novels are marked with arrival scenes in Moose

Jaw, Cardston, or Revelstoke. American immigrant novels, on the other hand, seldom extend further west than Sauk Center, Minnesota, and they are predominantly eastern- and urban-oriented.

A final difference of importance between the two "frontiers" arises from the fact that they were not settled at the same time. Technology meant that Canadian settlement, when it occurred, moved more rapidly, so that the various frontier "stages" which did exist were telescoped. Canadians could benefit from American mistakes, not only in adaptation to sod huts and barbed wire but in land ordinances, reservation administration, and power projects. Indeed, a Canadian frontier of the North exists today and will for many years to come. This northern frontier is not particularly western, either, for many areas of future development lie in northern Quebec, in Labrador, and in the eastern parts of the Northwest Territories.

The states which emerged from the American frontiers, whether of the Old Northwest, the Old Southwest, or the Trans-Mississippi West, passed rapidly through the equivalent of decolonization. Once they had achieved statehood, they could, within the limits imposed by a written constitution and the Bill of Rights, become social laboratories. That residual powers would shift, by Supreme Court decision, from the states to the federal government was true, but each state remained a reflection of a North American-based government, and, often, a relatively pale reflection, as one state became a theocracy, another an oligarchy, and yet another a highly progressive democracy. The channels for deviation from normative political standards were more circumscribed in Canada, for, under the British North America (BNA) Act of 1867 — the basic Canadian constitution (to which a Bill of Rights was not added until 1960, and then not entrenched) — residual powers flowed in the opposite direction.

Further, Canada as a whole was a stalking horse for an empire, and its frontier had to be viewed, politically as well as economically, as a cutting edge for change which, until 1867, basically originated in Europe, and even after 1867 still did so to a considerable degree. Most of the precedents by which a colony moved from that status, through representative to responsible government, and so to full independence within the Commonwealth, either arose from a Canadian situation, were tried in Canada first, or were demanded by Canadians. The United States became independent by revolution. The revolution itself was, in numerous ways, a product of the American frontier. Canada became independent by evolution. That evolution provided a different ethos, and the evolution was tied to Europe. Just as Canadian encounters with Indians were shaped in part by imperial regulations meant to govern diverse situations in Australia, New Zealand, or India, so were all aspects of the Canadian encounter with the New World. As the first Dominion, as the North American preserver of European values, however transmuted, Canada's self-image of its future and of its past differed from the American self-image. In the United States, the visible symbols of the past — the living evidence of what a people most wishes to believe of itself — would be codified under the National Registered Historic Landmarks Act of 1960. Three types of historic site would far outnumber all other kinds: those relating to the settlement of the eastern seaboard, those relating to the Civil War, and those relating to prospector and sodbuster, Indian and cavalryman. In Canada, the scenes memorialized by the National Historic Sites Board of Canada were, numerically, dominated by Loyalist sites, by east-coast and fur-trade settlements and factories, and by constitutional and legislative precedents. Few sites from the Canadian West were honoured, for the western or even the frontier experience had bitten less deeply into the Canadian consciousness.

Compared to the American, then, the Canadian experience lacked options. The counter-thesis of Canadian scholars, that great Laurentian thesis put forward by Harold Innis and by Donald Creighton, while also geographical, and in that sense comparable to Turner's, permits few options to Canadians. Creighton and Turner were not determinists of the simpleminded sort, of course, and they were not saying that one single factor shaped Canada or the United States wholly. But they did argue that these factors defined the channels in which the Canadian and the American experiences took place. However viewed, the Laurentian analysis did not lead to a thesis of optimism. It was not a thesis that would invigorate a people to assume that the future was theirs.[8] At no time did Canadians ever feel that they enjoyed security, not to speak of "free security", for the standard view of Canadian history was that Canada had moved more slowly towards independence than it otherwise might have done in order to retain the British tie as a makeweight against the gravitational pull of the United States. Against this was set the countervailing fear that Canada was being sold on the chopping block of Anglo-American harmony. Pessimism triumphant! Thus the fundamental interpretations of Canadian history at once suggested that Canada's future was limited, that Canada's options were few, and that Canada's greatest risks came from Britain and the United States and not from within, so that Canada was preoccupied with a binocular view of the world.[9]

Let us turn now, and more briefly, to the second of my attempts at an example of comparative history. To do so, I move away from comparisons between the United States and Canada to look to comparisons between Canada and Australia and, to a greater extent, New Zealand.[10] Again, we are examining genuinely comparable societies in that they were founded at approximately the same time, under the impact of much the same technologies, and — setting aside French Canada — from the same imperial stock. This comparative example is more an aspect of imperial history, another context into which the Canadian story must fit, than of North American history.

I begin with an assertion which, had I space, I am confident I could sustain. It is an assertion about the comparative history of race relations, and it is this: If four of the major fragment societies — those countries which were formed, in modern terms, from the transplantation of Europeans — in which settler groups came to form the majority of the population were put onto a comparative scale with respect to the degree of racial accommodation struck with the indigenous peoples, we would find that the harshest race relations developed in Australia, the least harsh in New Zealand, and that the experience with white-Indian contact in the United States fell more towards the Australian side, and the experience with white-Indian contact in Canada more towards the New Zealand side, of the scale. (I omit South Africa, where white settlers have always been in the minority, and the case of the American blacks, who were not of the indigenous North American population.) Taking this as my hypothesis, as it were, I must then put the question as an exercise in the comparative perspective — Why should such differences in settler-indigenous relations have existed?

There were, I believe, four major considerations at work which helped to determine the differential nature of relations between the encroaching white-settler peoples and the indigenous populations in these four examples. (That there were differences seems indisputable to me. The person who thinks that all white-settler, encroaching groups were alike — all rapacious imperialists — is, to my mind, as guilty of racist thinking as the person who thinks, or thought, that "all natives are alike".) Other considerations which may at first appear to be distinct, can, I think, be subsumed under the four which I want to examine here.

The first factor at work, obviously enough, is the nature of the white settlers. Now, white settlers differed, and markedly, from time to time and place to place, and their motivations for going to one colony or another also differed. The skills and attitudes they took with them differed depending on the point of technological change Britain had reached, on their position in British society, and on the unique skills they had acquired in relation to the act of settlement. The attitudes carried into Canada during the period (roughly 1815–1830) when Britain was "shovelling out paupers"[11] were quite different from the attitudes of the New Zealand settlers who paid their own way, who saw New Zealand as a positive goal rather than a negative escape, and who were seeking to recreate what they thought was the best in British society. Having different conceptions of themselves and of their purposes, they would apply different attitudes towards those native populations they encountered. If one intended permanent settlement, one might attempt to co-operate with the aboriginal society, if only for the purpose of turning it into a reservoir of cheap labour. Equally, one might wish to remove the aboriginal society because it competed, or potentially could compete, for the land on which the settlers intended to live permanently. Nor might land be the primary issue, for, depending upon the prevailing technology and the nature of the demands of world markets, other resources might be the primary targets of settler-indigene competition. Each high-technology culture perceives the role of technology differently, places different values upon specific aspects of technology, and conditions those who go overseas in the service of that technology differently. Within a managerial group the nature of interaction with the local culture will vary depending upon such matters as the generation, training, marital status, income, rank, expectations, and goals of those sent out.

To contrast Australia and New Zealand: The first settlers to go to Australia did so, for the most part, against their will, as convicts who lived under coerced conditions. Often illiterate and brutalized, they were ill-equipped to find any values in the aboriginal population, unread (even in Biblical charity), and little given to accommodationist practices in personal relations not to speak of interracial ones. Most probably they had never heard of the *beau sauvage*, and they certainly were not inclined to romanticize the native peoples with whom they made contact. The New Zealand settlers, on the other hand, were quite possibly among the best educated ever to go out to a colony. Many had been Chartists who were determined to recreate an Arcadian garden in New Zealand. Others were merchants and farmers who were literate and reared to the Bible, or, at the least, to read newspapers. Yet others were fully familiar with the idea of the noble savage and prepared to encounter him in the far reaches of the Pacific. Virtually all were in New Zealand because they had chosen to be there, and the coercive elements in their society were relatively few. Most had, after all, come in groups as an organized community, having paid either the whole or at least a major portion of their own passage. While all Australian settlers were not drunken rapists, and all New Zealand *pakeha* were not Rousseaus, or possessed of the kinds of college degrees needed today for a Jamaican to gain entry into Canada, there was a very real distance between the two groups of settlers as intellectual and social types.

A subsumed aspect of the question of the nature of the white settlers is, then, "What images did they carry with them by which they prepared themselves for meeting the indigenous population?" The answer in the Australian case is, virtually none. The answer in the New Zealand case is far more complex, and requires a diversion into the history of exploration and of race thinking prior to the 1850s.[12]

The entire history of exploration is one of fabrication and invention, rather than of the scientific unrolling of a map. The latter was the case for those inclined to think scientifically, to be sure, and in time fewer and fewer blank spots appeared on the charts of the voyagers. But most people prefer a good story to a colourless fact. Many of the maps of the fifteenth century had intentionally omitted islands for fear that crews might mutiny on long water passages and force pilots to turn towards them if they discovered their existence. How many people later saw these deliberate falsifications and — ignorant of their purpose — read their knowledge of the seas from them? Most of the captains and crew were eternally tired, often ill, certainly seasick, and in a state of barely controlled fear. How many of them could be expected to observe accurately whether the Maori who came down to the shore to greet Abel Tasman (who prudently drew no closer) were, as they reported, eight feet tall or not? As J. R. Hale has pointed out in an elegant little book on Renaissance explorers,[13] one of the chief driving forces behind the men who voyaged into the unknown was personal glory, and virtually no one who has sought glory has ever been an astringently accurate reporter.

The first achievement of the explorers was to make the world's terminology European. Not only were the Middle and Far East "middle" and "far" with respect only to Europe, but the many capes, bays, mounts, and rivers which testify to the saints of the Europeans' god in South America, Africa, and the Pacific showed who was in command of moulding knowledge. He who arrives first tells us what to expect, and who is there to doubt today that the moon is as Neil Armstrong says it is? To implant Europe upon the globe was to implant oneself as well. As Richard Hakluyt noted of Frobisher, whose Bay testifies to the truth of the observation, exploration and discovery were "the only thing of the world that was left yet undone whereby a notable mind might be made famous and fortunate". Accepting Christianity and their superiority as one must accept a mathematical given, the explorers were the Common Readers of their time.

Hakluyt's collection of voyages, issued in 1600, was only the greatest of many — and a bit more accurate than most. The printing of voyages, like prison-camp escape stories after World War II, provided a cycle of tales no less impressive than those of Canterbury. Ludovico Varthema, sailing from Venice in 1502, ultimately to reach Malacca on the

Malay coast, was "determined to investigate some small portion of this our terrestrial globe"; and Shakespeare, not alone in *The Tempest* but in *A Midsummer Night's Dream* as well, helped settle this determination upon those who stayed at home. The legends of medieval travel soon became the facts of the time. Fortunate Isles abounded, fountains of youth sprang from the savannah, Hindu temples showed unmistakable signs of early Christian influence since it was known to all that saints had passed that way, the Sargasso Sea reached up to claim its victims, the Kraken awoke, Amazonian women anticipated Wonder Woman, and the Anthropophagi reigned. One does not need Sir John Mandeville, for even so clear-headed an observer as the good Pigafetta, who returned from the Philippines after Magellan's death there, reported upon East Indians who stood not more than eighteen inches high and who had ears so long that one was a mattress and the other a cover when they slept. From Aruchete to Fu Manchu, and even to Doctor No, is not a long voyage.

For sentiments which today would be seen as unmistakably racist lay behind these visions of strangeness. Savages were noble, for they were innocent, but they were ignoble as well, ignorant and unclean. Today there is much new evidence on the old debate concerning whose gift syphilis was to whom, and while it appears that we need no longer accept that it was "white man's disease" in origin, an East Asian locus now being posited, it undoubtedly was the white man who carried the disease to the innocent who, in having it, soon were the ignorant and the unclean. Cause and effect were unclear. Natives did not feel pain, the seamen thought, and tested this notion from time to time. Natives did not grasp the relationship between intercourse and pregnancy, it was said — a happy vision of innocence later taken up by anthropologists who failed to associate myth with reality as those so-called ignorant natives did, but who rather chose to apply European ideas of myth and reality (as

Edmund Leach has so persuasively argued in *The Genesis of Myth*). Racially different, those of yellow, black, or brown skins who once held romance in their loins for homesick seamen later became the Yellow Peril or the black horde that might inundate Australian innocence, the bastard combinations of Chigroes who, Ian Fleming would tell us, were bred to kill virtually without thought because virtually incapable of thought. An Oddjob indeed.

Even those explorers who sought to hold to the hard bone of reality could not resist overpraising that which they saw. After all, one would wish to go voyaging again, and one's sponsors must be told of the attractions the future held, if not up this river then up the next. (Travel books today in no wise differ, for all inns are quaint, all beaches crystal, and all winds warm.) A rose was never a rose nor a rose, for it was always at the least an unconscious metaphor for something else, white herons the harbingers of the Fortunate Isles, birdsong the sounds of an approaching Heaven, a branch afloat in the sea advance notice of a continent over the horizon, a feather cloak proof of an empire built upon gold. Ultimately Montezuma's feather cloak, seized by Cortez, would come to rest in Vienna, where it remains today, a proud display of a heartless pillage, but the priest-kings themselves would be less tangible and further into the hills. All was beautiful, all was savage, and, because savage, beautiful.

But let us not belabour these Marvellian green thoughts in a green shade. Familiarity bred more romance, not contempt, and the many reprinted editions of the voyagers' tales came down little challenged to the nineteenth century — the Maori at least six and not eight feet tall but no less noble for that — to become the foundation for others who would help discover the *beau sauvage*. The British Empire itself was, some thought, both *beau* and *sauvage*.

Or at least so felt those New Zealand settlers (my great grandfather-in-law among them) who made the long voyage to the southwest Pacific. I belabour the point when I say that the white settlers of New Zealand found what they expected, that the white settlers of Australia also found what they expected, and that what they expected differed remarkably. Such is the nature of myth.

Obviously, then, the second factor at work is the true rather than mythical nature of the indigenous population, and the extent to which it did or did not fulfil those strange expectations. Even British settlers did not assume that all native people are alike, Philip Mason notwithstanding[14] (it is he who suggests that settlers shared a kind of Peter Pan myth to the effect that natives did not suffer, grow old, shed tears, or have a capacity for organized work. After all, we know that Mary Martin has aged for we have been around to see it). Again, in describing the indigenous populations of Australia and New Zealand I must over-simplify.

The aborigines of Australia, small and dark-skinned, were the very images of what the prevailing aesthetic mythologies of race thinking in Britain held to be ugly. They were an unattractive people. Furthermore, they had no apparent social organization, no apparent art, no cohesive religion; they were nomadic; they had nothing that Victorians or pre-Victorians could seize upon to interpret as worthy of attention. In short, they could not command the respect of the settlers, and especially not of the particular settlers who were coming, who were — as in the United States — inclined to think of native societies as worthy not of study but merely of removal.[15]

On the other hand, New Zealand settlers encountered the Maori, the most complex indigenous society in the South Pacific, who lived in settled villages and behind fortified walls in *pa*, who had a highly developed religion which was also visible, in the western sense, in that they could be seen being "at" their religion. They had a highly developed art which expressed itself in handsome wood carving, well-developed dances, and greenstone ornaments. The Maori on occasion fought wars in the European manner, even to the point of declaring truces upon the battlefield. They were the very image of the noble savage, conforming, for some, to a positive set of biases. Am I perhaps being Turnerian when I pose the first two factors then? — what was the cultural baggage that the white settlers themselves brought with them; what was the cultural nature of the indigenous group they confronted?

The third of the variables is the nature of the landscape in which the confrontation took place. Australia was a continent. On a continent one may make one of two decisions — to postpone any application of the final solution (I use the term deliberately), or to move as quickly as possible to an ultimate resolution. In Australia the decision by and large was to move to that final decision. In Tasmania, Tasmanian aborigines were tracked down with hunting dogs, and the Tasmanians were wiped out in a war of genocide, the last dying in her native land in 1876 — the same year that the Sioux annihilated George Armstrong Custer and his command at the Battle of the Little Big Horn. On the Australian mainland, the aborigine – now called the central-Australian aborigine — was made truly central by being pressed into the interior of the continent.

In New Zealand, which consists of two smallish islands, the settlers were faced with the same question and different voices posed the same solution. Time was short, however, and the settlers could not postpone for long, because white settlement was encroaching rapidly upon traditional Maori areas. A decision had to be reached much more consciously. The decision might have been different had the settlers been different, or had the indigenous group been different: it might have been for a war of genocide. But, given the first two factors and the nature of the landscape — which forced an early decision — the decision ultimately was in favour of racial accommodation, and this despite a series of Maori wars.[16]

The fourth of my factors is an external general question. What was the degree of commitment to retention of the area on the part of the metropolitan (or federal) government? The commitment in New Zealand was not very great. In the midst of the most bitter of the Maori wars, the New Zealand settlers found the British government moving into its Little England phase and withdrawing the imperial troops who were fighting the war. There is a great deal of difference between pursuing a war which is, for the most part, being fought for you by others and discovering that you will have to take up your musket and fight it for yourself. The New Zealand settlers quickly came to the conclusion that they did not care to continue the war solely for themselves, given the nature of the enemy they were facing. In Australia, the nature of the commitment on the part of the imperial government was different, making further postponement possible. Thus it is no surprise that in New Zealand the Maori would be given their own representatives in Parliament, while in Australia the aborigine was systematically denied access to citizenship.

What of Canada? Where does it fall on the scale? As in the United States, the nature of the settlers, the nature of the indigenous peoples, the nature of the landscape, and the nature of the imperial commitment led to a different conclusion than in either Australia or New Zealand. The conclusion Canadians know for themselves, from the Indian Act of 1876 — that interesting comparative year again — to the British Columbia Evidence Act of 1964. The latter act attempts to define an Indian or an Aborigine:

Any Aboriginal native or native of mixed blood of the continent of North America or its adjacent islands, *being an uncivilized person*, destitute of the knowledge of God, and of any fixed and clear belief in religion or in a future state of reward or punishment is an Indian. (My emphasis.)[17]

How many of us would be embraced by such a definition, destitute of the knowledge of any fixed and clear belief in religion or in a future state of reward or punishment? This kind of classificatory legislation comes so late to Canada because it, too, had the option to postpone any ultimate decision. In a continental-sized nation the Indian could be pressed, as in the United States, ever westward or onto reserves, so that it was not necessary to pose the question of survival in the brutal terms of genocide. Canada thereby postponed until late into the twentieth century what for others was a nineteenth-century decision, and is only now truly at the point of decision making — at a time when, given public sensitivities, the decision has a good chance of being made very differently than it would have been a century earlier.

Even on the Indian question, the Canadian-American relationship also was important. Not only could Canada postpone its decision; it could, to an extent, export it. The international border worked like a sieve, the Sioux, for example, grazing their animals on both sides of the border, but, with minor exceptions, fighting only in the United States. Indeed, from the Indian point of view there was no "Canadian Indian" and "American Indian", even if a long history of loose treaties dating back to the so-called French and Indian War showed that Indians were quite capable of entering into collaborator relationships with identifiable nationalities. The effect of postponement and export was, in a sense, that Canadians were, until recently, still working with nineteenth-century concepts of what an Indian is — witness that British Columbia Evidence Act, which was repealed as late as 1968.[18]

The function of this comparison, which has touched only lightly on Canada itself, has been both to demonstrate that comparison in itself is helpful in leading us to an understanding of *degree* — that is to say, of the ways in which we must qualify assumptions of generality or assumptions of uniqueness — and to say something of value about the Canadian experience. This second comparison is also meant to suggest that Canadian historians who have not looked elsewhere when examining the white settler-indigene question, or Australian historians who have not looked to North America, have placed themselves in so limiting a context of inquiry as to cut the historiographies to which they contribute off from the broad contact on which historiography must thrive. Put succinctly and in a cliché, he who only his own country knows, knows not his country.

I turn at last to my third comparison. I find it fascinating to examine the self-perceptions of cultures and sub-groups in terms of what they choose to take pride in and, in particular, what they thus seek to preserve from their past. The historical preservation movement is, to be sure, the product of middle- and upper-class societies; further, accident plays an important role in historical preservation, so that one is not examining purely rational processes in asking why place "x" or object "y" has been consciously preserved when place "a" and object "b" have been equally consciously destroyed. Commercial pressures, also, may aid preservation, if the site concerned is thought to have touristic value; or may work against preservation, where a new bank building or a parking lot will produce more dollars, pounds, or francs than a home lived in by one of the many Founding Fathers. Still, one can learn much about a people from what they offer up to succeeding generations as the visible symbols of their invisible past. This is especially so when historical plaques — taking up little space, innocuous, easy to ignore, threatening few commercial interests — are affixed (without preservation orders) to buildings, cairns, obelisks, and other concrete and stone underbrush, to mark the precise place where an event of importance happened.[19]

For what is interesting is seeing what different generations within different societies deem to be "an event of importance". Many people learn the little history they know from a casual encounter with an historical marker, and markers, plaques, and shrines form a public historiography for all to see. It is revealing to discover that the Nigerians have not destroyed Lord Lugard's office at Kaduna while the Ugandans have been rather harsher on his office at Kampala. The Germans, upon taking possession of Krakow in 1939, tore down the monument to Goethe (presumably because no figure of such importance to German *Kultur* could be thought to have lived in a Polish city); interestingly, the Communists have not put the monument back up, perhaps because they do not wish to commemorate a German? The infamous commandant of the Andersonville Prison Camp in the American Civil War is handsomely memorialized by Georgians at present-day Andersonville. The Malaysians debate blowing up A Famosa, the remnant of a Portuguese gate in Malacca, while the statue to Francis Light in Penang is put in storage. The British do nothing to preserve the site of the Battle of Bosworth Field; the Scots do much more at Bannockburn and Culloden; and the Americans most of all at Gettysburg and, of course, Yorktown. At the well-preserved scene of the most hideous prison and extermination camp maintained by Nazi Germany in Austria, the Austrian government has asked each government that lost citizens there to erect a memorial. On the banks of the great quarry at Mauthausen, where thousands died, there are many monuments which take as their theme forgetfulness and, on occasion, forgiveness. One, placed there by the Hungarians, states uncompromisingly, "Forget? Forgive? Never!" A very few miles away is Linz, where Adolf Hitler was born. There is no plaque of any kind noting that fact. All this tells us something, but what?[20]

In Britain there is little effort to preserve the exact site of a historically important event, partially because the English (in particular) conception of history is quite different from the North American. The time scale is different, of course, but there is more to it than that: the British have little metaphysical identification with a precise spot if that spot has been altered out of recognition, and they prefer to preserve a Great House for its architectural value rather than a field in which a royal crown may have rolled under a bush. North Americans place far greater emphasis on the precise place where, despite utter change, an event deemed noteworthy occurred.

There are now well over three thousand historic properties on the National Register of Historic Places in the United States.[21] Entry on the Register arises from a variety of possible nominations: state and county authorities, government agencies, interested individuals who can find broad support. In the last few years the bulk of such listings has tilted towards historic homes, but, until quite recently, those places defined as historic were strongly linked to American military history. For a people who have often declared themselves to be non-military, the preservation and demarcation of hundreds of battle sites and old forts reveals something kept hidden in the national psyche. The fact that the very spot in Fulton, Missouri, where Winston Churchill first publicly used the phrase "the Cold War" is now a national historic place suggests that it is the judgment of our generation that, for all time, the Cold War will be historically meaningful. What, then, of the plaquing of the site of the first gasoline station in the United States, at Signal Hill, California?

Consider the national historic sites of Canada. The first site was marked in 1922 (the first in the United States, in terms of federal administration of the site, was in 1890). No full document defining a historic site was generated at the national level in Canada until 1967. By 1971 there were 219 marked sites in Ontario, 103 in Quebec – apparently an indication that twice as much history took place in the one as the other? — and proportionately smaller numbers in all other provinces.[22] If one examines these sites *in situ*, or reads the texts of their plaques, one begins to grasp why the Canadian national anthem is so interested in having the loyal citizens of Canada stand on guard for thee. The greatest number of the sites by far are about Loyalists, or battles in the War of 1812, or Fenian raids, or — as with the plaque at Windsor, Ontario, at an alleged terminus of the Underground Railroad by which many hundreds of fugitive slaves sought refuge in British North America — assert a value judgment by implication: "Here," reads the marker, the fugitive "found in Canada friends, freedom, protection, under the British flag."[23] Put differently, at least a third of Canada's historic sites have been marked with plaques that are either explicitly or by broad hint anti-American in intent, reminding Canadians that they have been under almost constant threat from across the border. The famous undefended border (long shown by Colonel Stacey not to have been undefended at all) has been well defended by the text writers for the National Historic Sites Board of Canada.

An interesting conception of proportion also arises when looking at these plaques. There is one to the first cheese factory in Canada, the first butter factory, the first oil well, the first experiment with bird banding, and one to Sir John Carling. Americans, on the other hand, have placed a marker on the bridge in Santa Fe, New Mexico, where Fuchs appears to have given all those atomic secrets to the Russians. Does this all not suggest perceptions of history which differ? The Canadian perception, if one may use the markers as an indicator, is defensive, pacific, and given to honouring political figures. The American conception, it appears, is that history is a weapon for the future, aggressive, given to worrying about "firsts" and "mosts", yet one more way in which one may assert power. Here, too, Canada appears to have chosen a different path.

This last descriptive example, to my taste, is merely fun, even though it contains a serious intent. History need not be all high seriousness of purpose, for it is also casual, encountered in a walk on the street. The historian cannot cease being a historian, even when at rest, any more than the differences that set Canada apart from the United States can be eliminated by a ritualistic incantation of the charge of continentalism — a word that is not even part of the American's vocabulary, so that he literally is unaware of the word for what it is that Canadians fear. I have tried to suggest here, in part by indirection, that while Canadians do need to heed the injunction of their national anthem, they may have less to fear from without than from within, for the alleged similarities between the two nations — similarities which, some argue, would make it all too easy for the United States to absorb fragmented portions of a collapsing Dominion — do not outweigh the differences. These differences are real, they are likely to be lasting, and for the Canadian nationalist they are, or ought to be, comforting. Because Canada is different from the United States, because it is a superb testing ground for generalizations about historical development, because it has played so central a role in North American, imperial, and even United States historiographies, it is in the interest of Americans that it survive intact. Canada is essential to Americans, as a source of study, a source of contrasting knowledge about the use of the environment, about the impact of technology, about how people who share a continent may come to conduct their public lives differently from each other. If Canada did not exist, Americans would seek to invent it.[24]

PART II ♟ THE IDEA OF
THE MOTHER DOMINION

THE FIRST LINE OF THE DUST-JACKET COPY TO *SNOWBALL*, BY TED Allbeury, tells us that, "In 1940, FDR and Canada's Mackenzie King privately agreed to abandon the Allies if Hitler successfully invaded Britain."[1] *Snowball* is, we are told, a "novel of suspense". In fact, what is interesting and relevant here is that the author felt no need to identify Franklin Delano Roosevelt, but he did feel a need to provide identification for Mackenzie King. Yet once again the unknown Canadian was, if presented without his tag line, likely to remain unknown.

Precisely because Canada often feels neglected, its position in world affairs is an example of what political scientist Karl Deutsch means by national role playing. In his *Nationalism and Social Communication*, and elsewhere,[2] Deutsch draws upon Canada to examine the general way in which the citizens of a nation feel about their culture in relation to world affairs, rightly pointing out that Canadians have taken pride in being a peacemaking influence in the world, in being a golden hinge, a linch pin, and the Mother Dominion. The last self-conception, that Canada is the Mother Dominion, occurs in very few history books, the terminology more properly being the "first dominion", but the phrase "mother dominion" is common usage in Canadian newspapers, and it has led Canadians rightly to assume that much that is relevant to the emergence of constitutional precedence in other members of the Commonwealth arose first in Canada. All self-nominated descriptions, even if clichés, are well worth examining in terms of their popular rhetorical impact upon national self-consciousness. The notion of the Mother Dominion is rather more interesting than "linch pin" or "golden hinge" (although not more so than "Canada's century"), for it has the force of both myth — as in the case of the other journalistic catchphrases — and of fact. After all, it is true that most of the steps which the British government defined as essential to the process of preparation for independence (that is, for those societies which were consciously to go through such a process rather than resort to revolution), were derived first from a Canadian experience, created out of circumstances that first arose in Canada, or were established by a Canadian precedent. It is, simply, impossible to understand the notion of preparation and the way in which it was applied by British colonial administrators in the Gold Coast, or Malaysia, or even Ceylon (now Sri Lanka) without looking to Canadian history. Any scholar of African history unaware of the Canadian precedents seriously misunderstands one significant aspect of the process by which Nigeria or Kenya became independent nations.

Before turning to the application of the process of preparation — referred to in other contexts as decolonization — let me look for a moment at those who applied and interpreted the process, the colonial administrators in the field. One of the commonplace themes of British imperial history is that of the significance of "the man on the spot", that is, of the individual colonial governor, district officer, or advisor, who, by virtue of being present and having ideas of his own might well override both his original instructions and further communications from the Colonial Office.[3] In order to understand why a specific event occurred in the way in which it occurred in a specific colony, it is necessary to look to the man on the spot and to his often entrenched local advisors.

As training grounds, as stepping stones, as integers in a specified sequence of movement (or of promotion), certain colonies did play the role of intermediaries in the colonial process. *If* some colonial administrators did believe that all natives were alike, they came in part to this belief because of service in particular colonies under particular conditions;

equally, if others quickly perceived that all natives were not alike, this was in part so because they had experienced different groups under different circumstances. While Hong Kong and New South Wales and Ceylon all figure prominently in the sequences of posts for most colonial servants, and while the various West Indian colonies often were either the starting point or the point immediately preceding retirement for colonial officers, Canada more often than not played a crucial role in the shaping of attitudes towards the colonial service. Obviously J. F. W. DesBarres's failures as governor on Cape Breton influenced his mode of action as governor of Prince Edward Island, for he saw the latter post as literally "a second opportunity", where he might make recompense for what he had done, or had failed to do, on his "little isle of trouble".[4] Arthur Hamilton Gordon came to his noted dislike for representative and responsible government as governor of New Brunswick; knowing this, we can better understand why he resisted responsible government for so long as governor of New Zealand, or why he acted as he did when, as Lord Stanmore, he became High Commissioner for the South Pacific, based on Suva.[5] Sir Matthew Nathan's responses at Dublin Castle in 1916 were, in part, the fruit of experiences in Sierra Leone, the Gold Coast, Hong Kong, and Natal.[6]

Let us pause for a moment to look at one person, by way of example, in a little detail, and to look to the generality in a little depth. The one person is Sir William Francis Drummond Jervois, a figure so obscure his last name is pronounced differently in Canada, Australia, and Malaysia, three of his primary posts.[7] His chief significance to the historian of empire, no doubt, is that it was he who helped precipitate the Perak incursions by which Britain found itself drawn increasingly into a Forward Policy on the Malay Peninsula.[8] Jervois had been schooled in the Royal Engineers. The Straits Settlements, where he was based at the tip of the Malay Peninsula, at Singapore, was his first colonial governorship, for his previous highly successful service — in South Africa, in India, in Canada, in Britain — had been solely military and largely technical. Three experiences (which date from his military career), upon which he remarked in diaries and journals, deeply influenced his manner of conduct when he became governor, first of the Straits Settlements, then of South Australia, and, finally, of New Zealand.

The first experience occurred in South Africa. There, as a very young officer of the Royal Engineers, he was put in charge of the mapping of the territory around what is now Grahamstown. He helped open up the Eastern Cape, riding ahead of his survey team, often entirely alone, to scout out the low passes through the hills, and (a bit secretly) to make water colours of the terrain, for he had fallen in love with the landscape. One day he rode too far and was captured by what he referred to as some Zulu — almost certainly Khoi-khoi in fact — and was tied to his horse seated backwards, the horse then being driven into his camp. He later noted that this humiliation in the face of his own men had taught him that he must never again allow natives to gain the advantage of him.

The second experience took place in relation to Canada. Twice during the 1860s the British government sent Jervois to British North America, where he rendered two reports on the defences of Canada in the context of a possible invasion from the United States, where — by the time of the second report — it was seen that a Union victory in the Civil War was in the offing. Canadian politicians feared such an invasion, for they and the British government had been perceived in Washington to be pro-Southern, and it was widely rumoured that, on the one hand, if the North lost the war, the federal armies would attempt to seize Canada as compensation for the lost Southern states; if, on the other, the North won the war, the enormous federal army would seek revenge and expansion at the cost of Canada.[9]

Jervois was a courageous man. His excellent diagrams

of the defences of Boston's harbour, for example, were done on the spot, while rowing himself out into the harbour in a rowboat. A guard challenged him on one occasion, shouting, "What are you doing?", and Jervois, ever straightforward, replied, "I am making maps of the fort", to which the guard said, "Oh, that's fine", and let him go. This same lack of guile served Jervois ill, however, when he handed in his final report, for he concluded that Canada West simply could not be defended at all, unless the British government established naval control over the Great Lakes, which they were unprepared and probably unable to do. John A. Macdonald was horrified and angry, and when Jervois's second report was released in November 1864, a month to the day after the Fathers of Confederation had assembled in Quebec City to discuss a confederation, the Canadian and British governments fell into polite wrangling about their respective responsibilities for the defence of Canada. Jervois had recommended immensely expensive fortifications in his first report, and, while he pulled back somewhat from these in his second, he made it clear that without considerable sacrifice on someone's part Canada would have to rely on General Winter and a siege mentality to defend itself against the Americans.[10]

Jervois now found himself withdrawn from Canada, and it was always his belief that John A. Macdonald, displeased with the realism of his reports, had requested that the British withdraw him. Whether this was true or not, and it most probably was not in the sense that Jervois took it, the good colonel later remarked that he had learned in Canada that he must not give unpalatable advice to politicians unless he had the power to back his advice up through other politicians. He would remember this later when locked in battle with the Chief Justice of Singapore over the way in which he had disciplined a body of Nanyang Chinese, whom — he said — he would not allow to humiliate him. (With happy irony, the arrangement by which Britain had promised an imperial guarantee for a fortification loan, in order to realize Jervois's recommendations, was converted in 1873 into a loan guarantee for building the transcontinental railway; doubly had John A. Macdonald his victory over Jervois.)[11]

Jervois's third experience was in the Andaman Islands in 1872, where, as he walked behind and in attendance on the Viceroy of India, Lord Mayo, he was horrified to see a Pathan convict leap out and strike the Viceroy dead. This assassination came back to Jervois later when, as Governor of the Straits Settlements, he sought to avenge the murder of his emissary, J. W. W. Birch, by the followers of the Maharajah Lela at Passir Salak. Jervois's ultimate over-reaction was, in one sense, the long-range effect of his earlier experiences with natives, with politicians, and with death.

I turn back to the generality with some modest statistics to support my now obvious contention that a substantial number of high-ranking British colonial officers applied elsewhere knowledge which they gained in Canada. While much more research is needed into the backgrounds, marriages, career sequences, and promotion patterns of colonial officers, some facts are perfectly clear even without the aid of the computer.[12] Between 1783 and 1867, the governors of the various British North American provinces had served in fifty colonies prior to coming to Canada, largely in the West Indies. These same governors went on to fifty-four colonies, generally colonies of at least equal and often greater importance. The British North American experience frequently was a mid-point in the upward curve of service, and the knowledge gained from these one hundred and four gubernatorial experiences obviously was, in general, broadly applied. The patterns of movement are instructive. There was a tendency to bring from the West Indies those who had managed to learn French while there, and to put them into Lower Canada. There was a tendency to shift people directly from Nova Scotia to Upper Canada. There was a tendency to move people from Upper Canada to one of the Australian colonies. The Canadian experience was central, then, in the development of on-the-spot, even man-on-the-spot, administrative expertise.[13]

Now, what of the process to which such men applied themselves? What of the actual stages in the growth of autonomy? What steps were involved in the long trek through that textbook cliché, From Colony to Nation? Examine for a moment a book much used in the high schools of Ontario, *How Are We Governed?*, by John T. Saywell and John C. Ricker. This book lists twenty-two precedents or stages in the growth of autonomy by which a colony became an independent nation. All but three of the stages of which imperial constitutionalists generally write are on this list, which follows:

1846 Governor instructed to introduce responsible government.
1849 Lord Elgin's signing the Rebellion Losses Bill confirmed responsible government in Canada.
1858 Galt's Tariff established Canada's independence in economic affairs.
1867 Confederation—the beginning of a nation.
1871 Withdrawal of Imperial troops from Canada.
1880 Appointment of a Canadian High Commissioner to Britain.
1887–1911 Imperial and Colonial Conferences.
1904 A Canadian commander appointed for the Canadian militia.
1909 Creation of the Department of External Affairs.
1914 Canada determined the extent of her participation in World War I.
1917 The Canadian Corps placed under the command of Sir Arthur Currie.
—— Imperial Conference on the nature of the post-war Empire.
—— Formation of the Imperial War Cabinet with Dominion Prime Ministers as members.
1919 Canada asserted right to sign peace treaties.
—— Canada became a member of the League of Nations.
1922 The Chanak crisis determined Canada's right to be consulted in British foreign policy proposed for the Empire.

1923 The Halibut Treaty with the United States, the first treaty signed between Canada and a foreign nation.

1926 The Balfour Report to the Imperial Conference gave a definition of the modern Commonwealth.

1931 The Statute of Westminster removed all signs of colonial subordination.

1939 Canada declared war on Germany independently of Britain.

1949 Appeals to the Privy Council abolished.

19— Passage of BNA Act by Canadian Parliament and constitutional amendment in Canada.[14]

Missing here is the "Prince of Denmark", the Durham Report, of which more later, and also missing are those other three commonly accepted precedents: that a Dominion may remain neutral in a war in which Britain is engaged (Ireland); that, at the moment of independence, membership in The (British) Commonwealth of Nations is not a required intermediary stage (Burma); and that one may be a republic and yet have the Queen be Head of the Commonwealth of which one is a member (Ghana). To these some might wish to add India's assertion that "British" should no longer be part of the title of the Commonwealth, or South Africa's discovery that a nation may withdraw — or be pressured — from the Commonwealth.

It is not necessary here to rehearse the significance of each of the stages on Saywell and Ricker's list, for all are well known — or ought to be well known — to any student of Canadian or imperial history. The merest reminder should be enough, for those who have managed to avoid the study of Canadian history. Canada was the first colony in which the Governor was instructed to introduce responsible government, the first in which a tariff inimical to Britain's metropolitan interests was allowed to stand by the Privy Council, the first to confederate, the first to appoint a High Commissioner (rather than Ambassador) to Britain, the first to create its own department for external affairs, the first to declare that it would not automatically supply troops when

Britain found itself in a crisis, the first to sign a treaty with another nation, the first to appoint an Ambassador outside the Commonwealth, and so on.

Some of these "firsts" are more significant than others, of course: I place far higher value on the Galt Tariff of 1859[15] than do most imperial historians, for the wording of Alexander Tilloch Galt's response to the British government when challenged on his intent seems to me to be a crescendo of particular brilliance. On October 25, 1859, he wrote:

[T]he Government of Canada . . . cannot . . .in any manner waive or diminish the right of the people of Canada to decide for themselves both as to the mode and the extent to which taxation shall be im- posed . . . even if it should unfortunately happen to meet the dis- approval of the Imperial Ministry. Her Majesty cannot be advised to disallow such acts, unless her advisers are prepared to assume the administration of the affairs of the Colony, irrespective of the views of its inhabitants.[16]

Galt was an early student of geopolitics, long before Sir Halford John Mackinder had coined the phrase, for he recog- nized that only a transcontinental railroad line would guard Canada against the drain of American tap lines thrusting up from the south. Galt appears to have imbibed Henry Clay's ideas about the appropriate function of a tariff, for his tariff was the first framed in Canada with the avowed purpose of developing home industry. It incidentally angered the United States, which had entered into a reciprocal trade agreement in 1854 — the first reciprocal agreement ever negotiated by the British on behalf of a colony — and it nerved New Brunswick to raise its own tariff in 1860.[17] The magnificent effrontery of Galt's statement, with its strategically placed and almost snide "should unfortunately happen" and its warning that Britain might be faced with the necessity of direct intervention is as close to an overt declaration of in- dependence as Canadians ever made. Typically, the British government never offered a direct response to Galt's statement, at least until 1920 when his tariff was related to the Fiscal Convention of India.[18] All was a process of evolution.

The nationalism of a society that attains political independence through evolutionary stages is necessarily different from the nationalism of a society which attains independence by revolution. The latter knows the precise point in time when, by common historical consent and frequent patriotic reassertion, it achieved nationhood. Periodically, I teach summer school in an (always different) Canadian university, usually to a class filled with Canadian high-school teachers of Canadian history. At the outset I ask these teachers to tell me when Canada became independent. The teachers never fail to nominate at least three dates, and to my mind they omit the most interesting one. Most will name 1867, the moment of Canadian Confederation. But Canada manifestly was not independent at that point, as a glance at the Saywell and Ricker list and a resort to common sense with respect to defence, land, excise, and foreign policy will show. Others choose 1931, when the Statute of Westminster repealed the Colonial Laws Validity Act of 1865 and gave force of law to the statement, contained in the Balfour Report of 1926, that Great Britain and the Dominions were "autonomous Communities . . . equal in status, in no way subordinate one to another in any aspect of their domestic or external affairs, though united by a common allegiance to the Crown. . . ."[19] The third set of teachers split their votes among two or three of the other items on the Saywell–Ricker shopping list. (For myself, I think it not unreasonable to suggest that Canada was not provably independent until 1939, when it did that which it could not do in 1914, and declared war on its own behalf. Until a state has demonstrated, rather than merely asserted, that it alone has the final authority over whether or not to send its citizens potentially to their death, I find it difficult to argue that the definitions of independence have been fully served.)

The point here, however, is not to ask which date is the most nearly accurate from a constitutional or political point of view, but to suggest that when a people literally do not know when they became independent, their view of the process of governance, of law, and of what is meant by independence is likely to differ from that of those who are certain of the precise moment when they leapt full blown from the head of Zeus. Not only does the United States insist that it can identify that moment — July 4, 1776 — but Americans have by convention agreed that they were independent on the date that they asserted they were, not on the date seven bloody years later when Britain conceded the fact. The dates on the Saywell–Ricker list, while all of Canadian origin are none the less defined and agreed to by British historiography, so that the very process of decolonization was one which, while taking place on a Canadian stage, was at least as British in its metaphysics as it was Canadian. The aggressive American assertion that a declaration alone achieved the fact of which it was a harbinger takes place in the context of a single, nationalist historiography. Evolution implies trial and error, and it contains more than a hint of the conservative's need to see life as a minefield through which one picks a way carefully; revolution sees life more as an environment which one may batter about with one's elbows until it takes the shape one wants or has theoretically predetermined.[20]

To this point I have omitted that precedent which launched Canada's claim to be the First or the Mother Dominion: the Durham Report. Lord Durham's *Report*, as Gerald M. Craig has noted in his commentary on it, occupies "a central place in the history of the Commonwealth of Nations. . . ." It is "one of the most vigorous and perceptive expositions of the principles and practice of free government in the history of the English-speaking peoples".[21] The Report's greatness lay in the fact that it allowed Canada "to develop her identity to the full . . .".[22] The success of the grant of responsible government that flowed from the Report was "the direct justification" for the "concession" of this type of administration to the Transvaal in 1906 and to the Orange River Colony in 1907.[23] The Report became "the greatest constitutional document in British colonial history".[24] Thus stands the conventional wisdom on the Report, not necessarily wrong for having become conventional, into the 1970s.

Durham came to North America assuming that he was to examine a contest between a popular body fighting for free government and an executive rigidly upholding the Crown's prerogative. He thought in terms of cliché, and he came expecting to find cliché. What he found, he said, was two nations warring in the bosom of a single state; he found a struggle, not of principles, but of races. For this he in the larger measure blamed the French Canadians. The English were practical, forward-looking; the French were opposing all that was modern. (The hints of a kind of pre-Turnerianism here seem to me quite clear.) The fault, Durham thought, lay in a constitution that defectively lodged irresponsible power in the hands of a small group of the Lieutenant-Governor's advisors, the Family Compact. The partisan administration of the Governor, Sir Francis Bond Head, had heightened tensions. Urgency was added to the situation by the presence of the United States, a recurring theme in Canadian history. The solution seemed obvious: British institutions must operate freely within the colonies. Certain exceptions were to be made, and the idle and narrow notion of a petty and visionary nationality entertained by French-speaking Canadians ought to be discouraged. In time, if the various English-speaking colonies were to be united as one, the English would outnumber the French-speaking subjects; this too would become a common British theme, as when, well over a century later, Britain sought to neutralize Chinese influence in the proposed federation of Malaysia by including the Malay-speaking Borneo territories in the new nation.[25]

In this sense, the racial argument inherent in the Durham Report would be applied to other potential federations, in Central Africa, southern Arabia, Nigeria, and even the West Indies.

Perhaps the most instructive evidence for the relevance of the Durham Report arises in the history of modern East and Central Africa. While the report is not often cited by name, it is always present as the spectre at the dining table in many discussions, at Westminster, in Whitehall, in Nairobi, Kampala, Dar es Salaam, or Salisbury, of colonial policy for Africa. When Lord Salisbury declared in 1947, in a debate on Africa, that leading the colonies to self-government had been "the whole basis of British policy now for well over a century", the Durham Report was the reference point.[26] The recently published correspondence of Norman Leys and Dr. J. H. Oldham,[27] a spate of studies of Kenya in particular, and a most perceptive earlier article by Robert G. Gregory[28] show how the Mother Dominion figures in East African history.

After World War I, white settlers in East Africa began to speak of self-government, particularly for Kenya, which in 1920 became (except for a coastal strip) a Crown Colony. At the time there were between ten and twelve thousand Europeans in Kenya, perhaps twenty-three thousand Indians, and about three million Africans. During the early 1920s, the group usually referred to by imperial historians as the Humanitarians agitated for a change in the nature of government in Kenya. This agitation was led by the Archbishop of Canterbury, Randall Davidson, and by the London-based Secretary of the International Missionary Council, Dr. Oldham. They persuaded the Secretary of State for the Colonies "to emphasize African interests", and a major White Paper was issued by the Duke of Devonshire — who had returned to London as Secretary of State for the Colonies from his post as Governor General of India — proclaiming the doctrine of native paramountcy, asserting that "Ke-

nya is an African territory". While the unwary might pre-
sume this to be a notice to the white settlers that they should
not expect to remain permanently in Kenya, or that, where
the interests of native and immigrant groups conflicted, the
interests of the former should prevail, this was not in fact
the intent. Rather, Devonshire was hoping to undermine
Indian efforts at reform by showing that the twenty-three
thousand Indians were not Africans and that they had no
claims upon East Africa. He also wanted to destroy the
usefulness of East Africa as a base for the Indian sub-con-
tinental independence movement.

Control in the Colonial Office passed in due course to
another Conservative, L. S. Amery, who, in 1923, took up
the union theme from Durham, sensing that if Kenya, Tanganyika, and Uganda would unite, the Indians would be
outnumbered by the Europeans. The European community
would then be large enough to be viable and would be able
to embark upon the path to representative self-government.
In 1926, the Ormsby-Gore Commission advocated such a
union and explicitly championed European interests. The
next year Amery offered up the "dual policy", by which
African and European needs would be developed in comple-
mentary ways and the East Asians would have no significant
political role to play in the dual society. This White Paper
was in effect a return to Durham's policy.

Amery's argument had been formulated for him by the
then Governor of Kenya, Sir Edward Grigg (later Lord Al-
trincham). Grigg saw the Kenyan constitutional problem
(as he called it) explicitly in Durham's terms, and he sought
to prevent two — or more — nations from warring in the
bosom of a single state.[29] Soon Amery sent out another royal
commission to East Africa; this, the Hilton Young Commission, proved to be under the powerful influence of Oldham
and the Humanitarians, and the resulting report in January
of 1929 placed heavy emphasis on the notion of trusteeship,
of preparation for reversion of full rights to the indigenous

population, and of a subordinate position for Europeans. By 1930 the doctrine of native paramountcy had been re-affirmed.

What is interesting here is that both parties to the controversy were arguing out of the scripture according to Durham.[30] One emphasized what the famous Report actually said, the other the actual results of what Durham's report proved to be. Grigg quoted the Hilton Young Report with approval; it had made specific and favourable mention of Lord Durham's concerns. In short, despite the unfolding debate between Oldham and Leys — the latter a Christian socialist who had been a medical officer in East Africa for fifteen years — and despite the conflicting testimonies of Grigg, Sir Donald Cameron (friend of Oldham and Governor of Tanganyika), and the fifty-one individuals called to testify before the joint committee of Parliament charged with examining the Kenyan problem in 1930–31, an issue which appeared to be whether to renounce the Durham policy in favour of that advocated by the Humanitarians was in truth an argument over two positions generated out of the Durham Report. Among those who tried unsuccessfully to present their views to the Joint Committee was Johnstone Kenyatta who, later, as Jomo Kenyatta, would become the President of an independent, post-Mau Mau Kenya.

One of Oldham's hopes was that Britain would at last engage in systematic research concerning African governance and land holding. One result of this hope was Lord Hailey's famous *An African Survey*, first published in 1938 and subtitled *A Study of Problems Arising in Africa South of the Sahara*.[31] Again Durham sat at the banquet table, usually unmentioned, but, when Lord Hailey turned to the land question, once more explicitly embraced: "On the manner in which this [colonial administrative use of powers with respect to land] is conducted, all else depends."[32] Even after World War II, when Hailey prepared his as yet unpublished reports on Rhodesia and Southwest Africa, the presence of the hand of the "prophet of the modern Commonwealth" could be felt.[33] Nor was it a dead hand; for, once again, the Durham Report was taken as an alternative to revolution.

Yet heavy irony may rest over this recital of the ways in which a report generated to meet a Canadian condition was taken up to meet quite different if spuriously similar conditions in East, Central, or even Southern Anglophonic Africa. For the Durham Report may not have been what either school, indeed any school, of commentators and administrations have said it was. Recently two scholars, Ged Martin and John Manning Ward (both writing in Australia), have attacked the conventional wisdom about the Report and any extensions of that conventional wisdom elsewhere.[34] Both argue — Martin somewhat intemperately, but from a close focus on the Report itself; Ward more moderately, and from a broader view of the entire issue of colonial self-government — that British ministers could not have exported responsible government to the Canadas in 1840 because they themselves did not know what responsible government meant. Rather, Durham found that local politicians in Canada were determined to run things for themselves, and since Britain could not prevent their doing so, not having prevented analogous developments in the colonies to the south some sixty years before, the British sought to paper over their weaknesses through constitutional arguments. Durham, they suggest (although with different degrees of force), invented the principle that ministries would fall unless they commanded a parliamentary majority and announced that this was so. Ward suggests this was a prediction that proved true rather than a policy being transferred from Britain to Canada. All the more so, then, did Canadian circumstances come to dictate African cases.

Well, then, "mother" or "first" Canada may have been

in a number of ways. What of the second word to the phrase we are examining here? There is a well-understood and inherent awkwardness in the Canadian constitution, in the sense that the constitution *of* Canada (like the constitution of Australia) is in fact a constitution *for* Canada, being contained in Acts of the Parliament of "another country" — the United Kingdom. This is what the long debate over repatriation of the constitution was or is all about. Even with repatriation, however, the primary document itself, the BNA Act, would still be one that was initially passed elsewhere.

In the Colonial Conference of 1907 Sir Wilfrid Laurier attempted to do something about this subtle anomaly. At the time there were two commonplace usages of the word "dominion".[35] "Dominion" flourished as synonymous terminology, especially between 1900 and 1939 — Canada is no longer officially "the Dominion of Canada", but simply "Canada", all references to "Dominion of Canada" being progressively removed from the Acts of Parliament "as opportunity offers" since 1950 — for "self-governing states within the Empire–Commonwealth". "Dominion" appeared in the title of the King, as "of the United Kingdom of Great Britain and Ireland and of the British Dominions beyond the Seas, King". Australia, although progressively self-governing and a federation since 1901, was not a Dominion, having chosen a different term, "Commonwealth". In the royal title it seemed to many that "Dominion" was used in the sense of a colony, and this was an unhappy state of affairs for a variety of reasons, both domestic and foreign. There were too many Americans who still assumed that Canada was under the thumb of the United Kingdom and the terminology did not help to clarify the situation. Laurier readily recognized the problem, and, in 1907, spoke up:

I am not satisfied as to the words "Dominions beyond the Seas". It is a good expression, but I do not know that it is correct as it is used here .... I do not know that [such a phrase] may not include

Trinidad as well as Australia and Canada. It is not limited, so far as I can see, to the self-governing colonies.[36]

The New Zealand Prime Minister, Sir Joseph Ward, thereupon suggested that the phrase "self-governing Colonies" might be explicitly used, and Laurier countered with "self-governing Dominions beyond the Seas". Otherwise, he now added, the statement might even apply to Barbados! Laurier confessed that he would rather have liked the word "state", but the Australians somewhat irritatingly had already used the word for their constituent political units, whereas Canadians (as he pointed out) preferred "provinces" (which helped set them apart from Americans, who also used "state"). Laurier remarked that much confusion was inherent in the entire unsatisfactory situation. Alfred Deakin, the Australian Prime Minister, preferred "British Dominions possessing responsible government". Laurier stuck to his guns (even if the record dropped his capitals), "self-governing dominions beyond the seas", and recommended that they "sleep on it". They did not sleep on it, however, and Laurier, seeking a phrase that "we can then give out to the public", settled his mind upon "Self-governing Dominions".

Deakin then made a statement that may have confused many. "We [in Australia] recognise that the 'Dominion' is the senior of the 'Commonwealth', and therefore, the name 'Dominion' has a claim." Some hold that Deakin meant that Canada was senior to Australia, others that Deakin meant Canada was the senior member of the Commonwealth. Sir Kenneth Wheare, the leading student of such matters, concludes that the former was Deakin's meaning, and that he intended to indicate he would stand down on the basis of protocol if Laurier felt very strongly about the subject. Laurier concluded that he wanted a word not possible to define and remained adamant for "Dominion". The royal title continued to include the phrase "the British Dominions beyond the seas" until 1953, when it was omitted from the coronation ceremony for Elizabeth II.

In 1921, the ambiguity of vocabulary was pointed out by that master of the ambiguous, David Lloyd George, who asked in the House of Commons, "What does 'Dominion Status' mean?" Answering his own question (as was his custom), he replied that it was "difficult and dangerous to give a definition". It was important that he find one, however, because the question before the House related to the Articles of Agreement for a treaty between Great Britain and Ireland in which, Canadian precedent arising again, Ireland was to have "the same constitutional status . . . as the Dominion of Canada . . .". The Irish reasonably wanted to know what that status was. Lloyd George lamely concluded that: "Whatever measure of freedom Dominion Status gives to Canada, Australia, New Zealand, or South Africa, that will be extended to Ireland . . . ." So much for the definition and the debate.[37]

At the Imperial Conference of 1926, the problem was finally cleared up with that famous and ringing declaration that the Dominions were "autonomous communities within the British Empire".[38] This does not, of course, define "Dominion Status" as such, providing only an assertion — not without its own ambiguities — of equality with Great Brittain; nor did the word "Dominion" apply to Britain, reminding some correctly that, however equal all were in 1926 (or 1931), they had evolved to their equality by different paths. There were those who felt "Dominion" thereby retained a hint of subservience.

The French Canadians had never cared for "Dominion", and they found unsatisfactory the efforts to describe comparatively the function of the term without clearly defining it. In 1947, not for this reason alone, new letters patent for the office of Governor General replaced the words "Dominion of Canada" simply with "Canada". In any event, Canadians discovered that such their nation had always been officially, because upon closer examination the BNA Act (II, 3) revealed the words: "the Provinces . . . shall form and be One Dominion under the name of Canada." Perhaps all this discussion had not been necessary, for "Dominion" was not, in fact, a part of the nation's title. The pressing question of whether or not there was an implied subservience was taken up in 1944–45 by a Canadian, Professor F. R. Scott of McGill University; his articles were reprinted broadly in various Commonwealth journals, and they would be used in framing the Ceylon Independence Act of 1948 by which Ceylon did not pass through the intermediate stage of being styled Dominion — yet one other issue thus resolved out of a Canadian concern.

But a final paradox. On July 2, 1947, the British Government changed the title of the Secretary of State for Dominion Affairs (in order to recognize the realities of the Canadian, and by now Australian and South African, etc., situations) to Secretary of State for Commonwealth Relations. Yet, two days later, when the Indian Independence Bill was presented to the House of Commons, it established two new *Dominions*, India and Pakistan. These titles were changed when new constitutions came into effect, in 1950 for India and in 1956 for Pakistan, after which only New Zealand continued to embrace Dominionhood.

One of the problems with any evolutionary system of government is that somebody has to set the rules of the game. The course of upward movement on the rungs of Jacob's ladder will be measured by someone external to the process — that is, outside the colony in which mobility on the ladder is taking place. The external "objective" judge would, of course, be the British, who, if one did not play by the rules of the game, could always suspend the process — could always declare that a colony had not learned the next lesson of progress towards independence sufficiently well and must go two steps back down the ladder. The notion of evolutionary preparation, especially of a process clearly borrowed from someone else's success, would, for many African and Asian nationalists, contaminate the moment of independence. The very stages by which the glorious movement from colony to nationhood occurred — stages in which Anglo-Saxon constitutional historians took so much pride — were stages defined externally to non-Western cultures. Evolutionary steps towards independence were acceptable in the nineteenth and early twentieth centuries as most of the Western world was in the grip of evolutionary hypotheses. Today, more and more societies are gripped by revolutionary hypotheses arising from quite different if still Western sources. Canadians take pride in having not so much won their independence (which suggests conflict) as in having come to it by a rational, perhaps foreordained — for and by them — process. The Zulu are not likely to share this feeling. In Africa, the first generation of national leaders has been overthrown nearly everywhere, for, rather than being seen as the fathers of independence as Macdonald, Cartier, and Howe were for Canada, they are seen as the running dogs of the imperialists, having accepted the rules of the imperialist game. Only after the passing of the first, immediately post-independence group of nationalist leaders, followed by the rise of the "young Turks" — often in the military — would it be possible for non-Western societies to assume that they had overcome the stigma of evolution, that nineteenth-century principle of independence.[39]

Here, then, is a final irony. Canada *was* the First Dominion. The precedents developed within and for it, and in good measure by it, did help determine the path to independence of many other nations, since, in the process of decolonization, Britain chose to apply those precedents and to generate, from the step-by-step *ad hoc* measures first employed in Canada, a larger theory for later application in Ceylon or the Gold Coast. But in the final analysis, even though one cannot understand British actions in Kenya without understanding the Durham Report, nationalist historiographers of Kenya and other non-Western societies will and do find the entire structure of constitutionalism represented by the argument I have rehearsed here a British — or a Canadian — structure which ultimately is not central to their own conception of their own history. Is a precedent that is not perceived to be a relevant precedent truly a precedent? We are back to that truism of the intellectual and social historian, that ultimately what matters most in comprehending human motivations is to understand what a people believe to be true of themselves and of their history, not what "the facts" objectively conceived may be. That Canada *was* the Mother Dominion is demonstrably true; that many Canadians take pride in this truth is evident; that this truth is merely an idea, and no more, for most of the former British Empire is no less true.[40]

PART III ♘ THE IDEA OF
AMERICAN IMPERIALISM

AMERICANS CANNOT UNDERSTAND THEIR OWN HISTORY WITH-
out understanding Canadian history. Conversely, Canadians
cannot understand their history without understanding
American history. Some might suggest that this view repre-
sents a form of American intellectual imperialism, that it
does not let Canadian history stand on its own feet. Elsewhere I have tried to show a number of ways in which the
Canadian experience is relevant to non-Canadian histories.[1]
I have also suggested that Canadians are not in a good position to understand African and Asian nations that came out
of the British Empire, despite the Canadian belief that
Canada has been a linch pin, a coupling pin, between member nations of the Commonwealth and the United Kingdom.
The Canadian experience is highly relevant, indeed essential,
to the study of the British in Africa, but far less relevant to
an African nationalist perception of African history.

In many African and some Asian societies that "evolved"
out of the British Empire, it seemed necessary for "young
Turks" to overthrow the fathers of independence in order to
achieve for themselves and their countrymen a genuine
sense of national and intellectual independence. There was
a second scenario, of course, in which, in face of a threat of
being overthrown, many African leaders turned to dictator-
ship in order to remain in power. That is, they set out to
show that they were not running dogs of the imperialists,
and were not the captives of democratic liberalism, totali-
tarian democracy, or a Westminster model of Parliament.
The second scenario no less than the first flows from the fact
of imperialism. Once encountered, imperialism does not admit of much freedom of choice.

Nor does the existence of a very real American imperialism admit of any wide-ranging choice open to Canadians. I am not, please note, making a political statement when I say that America is an imperialist nation. Imperialism is a natural stage in the evolution of the relations between high-technology societies and lesser-technology societies. To this extent Lenin was correct: imperialism was and is inevitable. Imperialism is a descriptive word that should correctly and unemotionally denote the nature of the relationship that exists as divergences of technology broaden, as they invariably do before they lessen. Power by its nature can be shared but not equally shared; when equally shared, the condition that prevails no longer can be described as one of power. Imperialism is about particular ways in which power is employed.

Until recently Americans have fought shy of the term "imperialism". This is an indication of the power of that exceptionalist school of American historiography, the school of Frederick Jackson Turner and all others who sought to demonstrate that the United States was unique, that America is an exception, that Americans required a different vocabulary to describe their experiences. In American history textbooks, what I will call imperialism is labelled "American expansionism". The real difference between American expansionism and American imperialism is small (although both terms can be of value); the obvious difference in the emotive meanings for the American public is very large. Nuance is important here just as the difference between using "the conquest" and "the cession" for the events of 1756–63 is significant in Canadian history.

The failure of American historians to accept the term "imperialism", at least until recently, has meant that American scholarship on American imperialism has been highly parochial. Even more recent books, often said to emanate from some place occupied by a group called "the New Left", seem to me to exist in a conceptual vacuum.[2] While willing to use European (not necessarily Marxist) terminology, like imperialism, the New Left historians have none the less continued to travel down the exceptionalist road, for they appear not to have read the British, or the German, or the French literature on a subject about which, after all, these three nationalities have much experience.[3]

Properly speaking "colonialism", "imperialism", and "expansionism" carry somewhat different connotations in any event.[4] The first most correctly applies to the period of overseas settlement in plantation colonies (in the seventeenth-century meaning of the term), from — as dates of convenience — the opening of the Vasco da Gama epoch of Asian history in 1498 to the end of the American Revolution in 1783.[5] The second term temporally applies to the period since 1783. However, "colonialism" also tends to suggest outright annexation of a territory ("neo-colonialism", of course, does not), while "imperialism" embraces a variety of informal modes of dominance short of annexation. More than with the other terms, an element of racism is implied. Another distinction often drawn is that the first applies to white-settler activities in so-called uninhabited lands, while the second applies to economically exploitative activities primarily in Africa and Asia.

Whatever semantic confusions may arise, "expansionism" remains largely the possession of the Americans, although since it also is applied to the Russians and Chinese it serves the secondary purpose of meaning movement into contiguous territories often occupied by people of a different ethnic background. In the American case, moreover, the word has been used with equal force to describe the occupation or direct annexation of overseas territories ("territories" apparently being a neutral word that seems to suggest to those who use it that the area involved is unoccupied, or occupied by an unorganized society, or otherwise not a "state" or "nation", so that issues normally relegated to "diplomatic history" do not arise except when the "territory" is claimed by another high-technology power). By an easy acceptance of labels we avoid the realities. Expansionism and imperialism thus both embrace some notion of "informal empire" as well, in the sense that, while formal annexation may occur, it need not occur for the terms to apply. One can see why historians of the phenomena with which these words are identified find them inadequate to the historian's descriptive and analytical obligations.

With the emergence of the concept of informal empire,[6] it is recognized that a nation need not annex a territory in order to exercise imperial control over it. Indeed, as Latin American historians have often noted, there was a period of time during which Argentina was referred to as the sixth Dominion — at a time when there were five formal Dominions — because of the degree to which its economy interlocked with that of Britain. The extent of economic dependency of Uruguay on Great Britain in the nineteenth century was very similar to the economic dependency of New Zealand upon Britain in the late nineteenth century. Neither annexation nor settlement appear in and of themselves to make it possible to draw a valid distinction between informal and formal empires. If one is to study the impact abroad of a metropolitan economy, or the way in which an imperial nation manipulates the domestic politics of another society, then neither the act of annexation nor the act of settlement is essential to the study. There are useful comparisons to be made between Canada and Cuba in terms of staple dependency. There also has been a Canadian imperialism, as I defined the term, as evidenced by half-hearted efforts to acquire some of the West Indian colonies from Great Britain;[7] by Sir Wilfrid Laurier's obvious sense of distaste in 1907 that Canada, by being called a Dominion in a particular context, might be lumped together with Trinidad or Barbados, or that they might aspire within the same time frame to similar constitutional status; and, more recently, by the way in which Canadian banks have come to dominate the economies of the Bahamas and Barbados.[8] Virtually every high-technology society has engaged in informal imperialism.

The principal mechanism in informal imperialism is the development of a network of relationships which focuses on the concept of the collaborator, and which involves the development or extension of forms of dependency.[9] In this context and to the scholar, collaborator is not a pejorative term. The collaborator is not to be confused with the Quisling of World War II. Rather, the collaborator is parallel to and in some ways identical to the *comprador* of East and Southeast Asia.[10] Again, as with imperialism, reference to the collaborator matrix should not be charged with presentist political meaning, the rhetoricians of the political left notwithstanding.

Leninist interpreters of imperialism are not happy with the thesis put forward by Ronald Robinson and John Gallagher, the chief and first proponents of the collaborator theory of functioning imperialism, for it does not allow for a distinction they find important in futurist terms. An example of a good scholar who arrives at wrong answers is Harry Magdoff, who in a number of books has analysed the economics and the political and social consequences of the "new imperialism".[11] It requires a more highly trained eye than my own to be able to detect the actual as opposed to the asserted differences between the technological and social impact abroad of the capitalist bloc of nations and the technological and social impact abroad of the socialist bloc of states. As Magdoff and others[12] have persuasively argued, one "new" form of imperialism arises from foreign-aid programs, since such aid often extends rather than ends the dependency relationship. When strings are attached to the aid, as is often the case, a collaborator mechanism is inevitable. The conclusions are, I think, correct, although for the wrong reasons.

Certain ironies confront one almost at once. The first is that those scholars who are attempting to offer a global analysis of capitalism and competition in general, and of imperialism as a symptom, none the less continue to write from within the confines of a single historiographical tradition. Those who write on the politics of underdevelopment in Africa, for example, show little evidence of having read the work of the major Latin American dependency theorists. Equally, the Latin American scholars clearly have read very little about imperialism as it is now studied, and appear to be wholly unaware of the body of literature relating to the collaborator thesis. Now and then a single scholar, usually British, provides some sense of triangulation — D. C. M. Platt is the prime example[13] — whereupon no one else, Americanist, Latin Americanist, or Africanist, appears to take the message, and the broad theorists fall back into the cubicles which protect them from data which might challenge the breadth of their theories.

The lack of comparative perspective cripples the effectiveness of the analysis and results not in an economics of analysis but in an economics of resentment.[14] Time and again the data argue that a particular statement concerning dependency or class structure must be revised, and yet the founding fathers of the dependency or some other school of thought absorb the data without altering the conclusions. An excellent case in point is the work of André Gunder Frank, early and still perhaps chief analyst of "internal colonialism".[15] Frank sees cities as the locus of colonial domination. This is scarcely new, since the city almost always is the centre of technological forces. Further, national metropoles subject their hinterlands to "capitalist satellitization and exploitation". This is so because of the concentration of public and private investment in the cities, because of a regressive tax structure forced upon the peasantry by the more sophisticated city politician, and because of the transfer of economic surpluses from the outlying regions. One is tempted to ask, "So what else is new?" The temptation is more urgent, however, to say that an analysis of this kind, while perhaps correct for Brazil — to which Frank applies it — is of little utility in understanding the nature of, say, the Australian economy, and that it is dangerously optimistic in its implication that if one can bring to an end satellitization as Frank describes it, one will end exploitation. Lionel Tiger and Robin Fox would scarcely agree,[16] and nor do I. Even the more sophisticated and recent dependency theorists, with the important exception of Fernando Henrique Cardoso,[17] appear to be unable to escape from the ethnocentrism inherent in nineteenth-century Marxism. Dependency in fact suggests a reciprocal relationship, not unilaterally imposed from outside but taken up, if one may use the word, in collaboration.

Canada's staple dependency, the United States' exploitation of that dependency, and the satellitization of Canada by New York City are parallel assumptions to those made by the Latin American dependency school. There is a problem here, however, which arises from a second irony. The intellectual or the producer of hemp or the wheat farmer may or may not feel exploited. A sense of marginality may express itself in many forms. When dependency theorists argue that there is an asymmetry in urban-rural relations in Mexico, for example, and that the Indian and mestizo feel estranged from the nation, although in different ways and to different extents, the theorist is allowing what his system of logic dictates to him to intervene between fact (if it is a fact) and conclusion. As Richard M. Morse has noted in writing of this problem,[18] the Indian may not see the town as the agent of domination at all, but rather as the supplier of needed services, certainly commercial, medical, and technical, but also quite possibly educational and religious. Nor does the Indian necessarily assume that he must surrender his culture to the town, for he may feel himself to be intelligent enough to use the services selectively and with safeguards arising from within his own culture. The dependency theorist, the student of imperialism, who assumes that energy or leadership or coercion flows in a single direction is as guilty of a casual (and causal) racism as any nineteenth-century slave owner. As Morse has noted, when speaking of collective attitudes, the city is a theatre, not a player, "a node of forces, not a quantum of energy". National histories must not be reduced by culture-blind theoreticians into reflex reactions to external affairs; national histories also have their own internal dynamics.

With a quite different vocabulary, and using quite different case studies, this is precisely what Robinson and Gallagher have argued by creating their collaborator model. Here again one sees the irony arising from the self-chosen intellectual isolation of the dependency theorists, including the staple-dependency analysts of the Canadian condition. For the collaborator model is especially close to the heart of the problem of the relevance of American imperialism to the Canadian experience.

The collaborator argument runs approximately as follows. Imperialists, wishing to save themselves money and trouble, and needing to create conditions of stability from which they can establish predictive abilities and the future productive capacities of the exploited societies in order to make for effective policy planning generally, sought to cooperate with the elites within the non-Western societies. The goal was to work through the existing political and social structures. Of course, there might well be indigenous groups which, for local reasons, were challenging the traditional elites, and those groups would be likely to embrace the high-technology society in order to obtain the means to break into the monopoly of power. Those groups already locked into a dependency relationship with a traditional elite in pre-European society would be likely to accept European arms and other elements of European life, and to co-operate with the Europeans, so that the pre-European indigenous pecking order might be destroyed. Such displacement could occur without respect to European wishes. Those displaced would be angry with the imperialists, while those that had newly risen into elite positions might well be highly pleased with the imperialists and co-operate with them for reasons of their own. Therefore, if one is to understand imperialism one must study the indigenous society as closely as one studies the imperial power. If people collaborate, that act says at least as much about the collaborators as it says about those who subtly or crudely create the circumscribing conditions of the collaboration.

Implicit here is a call for an end to the idea of victims. One must cease looking at a minority group, a dependent state, or any collective entity as though its history were invariably a recitation of failure, a history of grievance. A form of racism lurked behind the once-popular assumption that these societies were always downtrodden because they lacked resources with which to resist, for in fact the black slave in antebellum America, for example, resisted in a wide variety of ways. One of the ways to resist was through collaboration, if one collaborated for one's own ends, perhaps in order to grow strong until some day one could throw the rascals out. One might collaborate, as one nineteenth-century Brazilian politician said, because he believed Great Britain to be the greatest liberal democracy in the world, the wave of the future, and he wished he were British.[19] One must abandon the assumption that one body is the victimized and the other the victimizer and look to the actual dynamics of the relationship. It does not help us to understand Canada to see it as merely or even largely a survivor, and Margaret Atwood's conclusion that the central preoccupation of Canadian poetry and fiction has been "survival and victims" strikes me as harmful.[20]

One reason some writers find the notion of the pure victim useful is that it lacks apparent ambiguity. Imperialism is fraught with ambiguities. Consider this one: Lenin predicted that the capitalist nations would make war upon each other, and that, through an imperial war, competing capitalisms and capitalism itself would be destroyed. The "new imperialist" school must account for the failure of such a war to have destroyed capitalism. One explanation is that the United States, by controlling multinational corporations, has eliminated the competition that induces war and now enjoys world economic dominance. Lenin, however, was moved to write his essay on imperialism because he disagreed with Karl Kautsky, whom he saw as a bourgeois revisionist, who held that there would be no war of international capitalism because one nation would come to dominate all capitalists. Thus the neo-Leninists, in order to reach towards Lenin's conclusion, must embrace reasoning similar to that against which Lenin wrote.

Just as it is difficult to identify precisely who the imperialists are, it is sometimes difficult to single out the capitalists according to the descriptions given of them by those who see them as a single community. As most students of history have discovered, the business community generally is opposed to war, to intervention, and, less generally, to foreign aid, for all that the happy businessman wants is a stable environment in which he can reap his profits. Wars introduce the unpredictable. To be sure, sectors of capitalism no doubt benefit from a state of potential hostility — that is, from arms races — but it does not follow that they benefit from war itself. Nor do all multinationals behave as International Telephone and Telegraph has done.

This intolerance of ambiguity manifested by the left is well illustrated by a recent small book, *Imperialism and the National Question in Canada*, by Leo Johnston, Steve Moore, and Debi Wells. There is, Johnston notes, "a growing and deepening division among left wing thinkers in Canada around the question of whether Canada is best described as a colony of the United States or an imperialist country in its own right".[21] Rather desperately the authors conclude that Canada must be one or the other. Of course, in some senses, Canada is in fact both.

The problem, then, as I have tried to show, is that there may be many different types of imperialism. Indeed, if one examines the ways nations which publicly oppose the role the United States plays in the world employ the term, one quickly discovers that each has invested the word with a meaning of its own. When the Québécois say that the United States is an imperialist nation, they mean something rather different from the Swedes when they use the word, or the Cubans, or the Nigerians, or, certainly, the Russians. To conclude that because all employ the same vocabulary they are condemning the same aspects of the complex American impact overseas is to simplify to the point of banality.

Some Canadians, for example, see American imperialism as arising from the ignorance of the average United States citizen towards things Canadian. This imperialism of ignorance is offensive, perhaps harmful to the national *amour propre*, and sometimes silly; it is not necessarily sinister. Everyone recognizes that Americans are far more ignorant of Canadian matters than Canadians are of American matters. In 1969 Nelson Rockefeller, then Governor of New York, introduced the Prime Minister of Canada, Pierre Elliott Trudeau, as married when he was not at the time; when he then also introduced the Premier of Ontario, John Robarts, with a French pronunciation, Rockefeller was widely condemned in the Canadian press. The press sought to reach the Rockefellers of the land to diminish their ignorance. However, the Rockefellers of the land did not have time to have their ignorance diminished, and they were in any event not guilty of imperialism as charged (at least on this evidence) but rather of sundry lesser offences: poor staff work, rudeness, taking on too much to do, ineffectiveness, inattention.

There is also the imperialism of indifference. Americans persistently ignore matters Canadians consider important.

Of course, New Yorkers ignore matters that Los Angelenos think important too. The charge of being indifferent to Canadian matters is a serious one when directed against the international marketplace in education, and the kinds of fears most loudly voiced by James Steele and Robin Mathews have a reasonable basis.[22] There is no question that a number of Americans filled departments of history, sociology, or political science in many of the newer Canadian universities at a time when Canada could not fully meet its own needs and that most of these American academics knew little about Canada even though they may have been teaching about a social problem with significant Canadian ramifications. For the class they usually chose American rather than Canadian examples, and some inveighed against the inclusion of sufficient Canadian content in the curricula of their departments. Surely any department that deals centrally with a nation's culture and heritage, as sociology, literature, and history do, must offer substantial Canadian content to its clientele. Americans ought to be interested in Canada in any case. But Steele and Mathews were attacking the wrong problem. They were attacking a numerical or statistical problem — too many Americans — rather than the intellectual issue — too many Americans who saw nothing in the reward structure that would induce them to learn about Canada. Even so, and supportive as I am of the righteous resentment felt by Steele and Mathews, I feel they ignored a point central to imperialism. Taking data from 1961, they projected to 1968 and found that 25.5 per cent of Canadian faculty were foreign born and the trend was up. Of course, a similar figure might have applied to other growth areas in the Canadian economy, for Canada had encouraged heavy immigration. The faculty of my own university, Yale, is 26 per cent foreign born, and great universities do tend to harbour high percentages of the foreign born, for they seek diversity as well as quality. At no time did it occur to the nation that because Yale's faculty was over a quarter foreign born it was failing to do its duty to American society.

There is also the imperialism of trend setting, by which what happens in America today is fearfully thought to be going to happen in Canada tomorrow. If there is murder on the streets in New York today there will be murder on the streets in Toronto tomorrow. One imagines a creeping virus labelled Americanism making its slimy way across the border. To what extent, in fact, does the United States provide a negative or positive model for the rest of the world? Prediction and evaluation are not the same, of course, and to conclude that an American trend will surface in Canada is not the same as arguing that the trend should surface. An examination of influence and trends may be salutary as well as instructive, for one may discover that the past cannot be changed. Recently, Richard Rose, an American teaching in Scotland, looked for American trends in Britain.[23] Often he found the label but not the trend, or the fact but not the influence. Good design, for example, can be present in Britain or in Canada without necessarily having been imported directly from Sweden or America. Years ago, Dennis Brogan remarked upon the European tendency to attribute the rise of juvenile delinquency in Europe to the American virus — shades of Talleyrand — when in fact what was happening were the normal social developments that so often accompany industrialization and technological change everywhere, developments which happened to have occurred first in the United States so that they were alleged to be American in nature.

There is also the imperialism of popular culture. Here is a favourite Canadian charge against Americans: they are the Republic of Junk.[24] Americans flood Canada with junk. The Americanization of the English language, the mediation of environments and of food technology, the onslaught of American advertising, the impact of American religious sects, popular music, jazz, television, movies, all are evidence of a superculture hustling mindlessly on the road.[25] Here, too, surely the theme of collaboration is relevant. The consumer is as much at fault as is the purveyor when junk changes hands. I do not see that it is a form of American imperialism if Canadian taste demands American products. Canada is a free country, after all. In a free society, citizens are free to show bad taste.

It is not my intent to trivialize imperialism and the sins it is heir to when I suggest that there also is an imperialism of the explanatory excuse. A society faced with intractable problems often looks outside itself for an answer to or for the alleged cause of those problems. Modern societies, faced with the problem of what Daniel Bell calls the assumption of rising entitlement amongst their citizens, often coinciding with and further fuelling a crisis of national unity, place the blame upon vast impersonal forces such as a malevolent imperialism emanating from elsewhere, forces which he calls sources of instability.[26] The existence of a problem that is deemed to be insoluble, or is asserted to be so by politicians and the press, is a cause of instability in the society. The existence of a parliamentary *impasse*, the growth of private violence, the destruction of civil liberties in order to put violence down, the disjunction of economic sectors within a society, multi-racial or multi-ethnic conflicts, the alienation of the intelligentsia, humiliation in war — all contribute to instability and all may be blamed upon someone else. Canadians, long convinced of their moral superiority to the United States, have, until the rise of the Lévesque government in Quebec, looked to the Republic as the source of their ills.

Finally (here), there is the imperialism of anti-imperialism, as practised by John F. Kennedy in the fine tradition of Woodrow Wilson. Perhaps this is the most subtle of all the forms of imperialism, the notion that Americans stand for freedom for all peoples, that they are a redeemer nation.[27]

Here is John Kennedy addressing the American Society of Newspaper Editors in April of 1961; the subject is going to the moon:

Those who came before us made certain that this country rode the first waves of the industrial revolution, the first waves of modern invention and the first wave of nuclear power, and this generation does not intend to founder in the backwash of the coming age of space. We mean to be a part of it. We mean to lead it, for the eyes of the world now look into space, to the moon and to the planets beyond; and we have vowed that we shall not see it governed by a hostile flag of conquest but by a banner of freedom and peace.... But why, some say, the moon? Why choose this as our goal? And they may well ask, why climb the highest mountain? Why, thirty-five years ago fly the Atlantic? . . . We choose to go to the moon. We choose to go to the moon in this decade, and do the other things, not because they are easy but because they are hard, because that goal will serve to organize and measure the best of our energies and skills; because that challenge is one that we are willing to accept, one we are unwilling to postpone, and one which we intend to win — and the others too.[28]

John Kennedy would not have seen himself to be an imperialist. He would not, unlike Lord Rosebery, have declared to the world that he was proud to be an imperialist. Indeed, officially the United States has long been anti-imperialist. As William Roger Louis has amply demonstrated, even in the midst of World War II it was official if undeclared American policy to work for the freedom of Britain's colonies.[29] Winston Churchill's famous statement that he would not preside over the dissolution of the British Empire was directed against Americans, not Germans or Japanese. In 1944 the British Colonial Office and Treasury exchanged a note recognizing American intent: "The Americans did not take advantage of the mounting wartime debt so as to control colonial economic development. The Colonial Office secured War Cabinet and Parliamentary approval of the Commonwealth Development and Welfare Act because Britain was the trustee of a great Colonial Empire. The Second World War witnesses a moral regeneration of British purposes in the colonial world." This was so in part because Britain recognized that the Development and Welfare Act was necessary in order to buy time and a lessening of pressure from the United States, which was particularly intent upon Indian independence.

Officially anti-imperialist or not, the post-war world soon thrust the United States into the role of dominant technological power, and, willy-nilly, America became an imperialist nation. In doing so, the United States transferred abroad its consumption technology, but it did not transfer its production technology. If its absolute contribution to the less-developed countries was positive, its relative contribution was negative. It created an imperialism of *inter*dependence.[30]

By this route we return to Canada. I have not examined here the usual arguments about the impact of American investments, or branch plants, or managerial hiring practices, or unassigned research allocations, because they are so frequently examined elsewhere. Though trite, many of the charges are true. Rather, I wish to emphasize the imperialism of interdependence. When, in 1911, the British government sent to Ottawa a cablegram that read in part, "Undejected acting miterone sluggard ticpolonga deplexam bootjack recent legislation recidiate reciprocal trade between Canada and Japan baptizing existing treaty expires orbibus jibcama. . . .",[31] the intent, expressed here in code, was to create a system of interdependence with Japan. This was done, and, in time, Canada found that linkage inconvenient, even dangerous, and broke it off. Collaborators in both societies worked to serve their own but also their nation's ends. Neither was victim, neither imperialist, unless both were both. So, too, would Canada develop an imperialism of interdependence with the United States. Perhaps in this way Canada would, to answer Leo Johnston's question, become an imperialist country in its own right;

perhaps Canadian socialists would need to overthrow the Canadian capitalist class — to promote socialism in one country — before they looked for larger fields to conquer. Whatever the case, however the terms might be manipulated, one could not avoid the conclusion that Canadians were real-life gun-slinging cowboys too; that the United States had no monopoly on imperialism; that the Canadians who, drunk on Strega, ran rampant one night among the fireflies of Naples in 1944 were part of a larger North American pattern of innocence, destruction, and unthinking exploitation.[32] Perhaps continentalism *had* triumphed. Certainly, and at the least, no Canadian could say, "You, American imperialist", without also saying something fundamental about Canada as well.

I do not mean to suggest here that there is not a very real American imperialism. Nor do I mean to dismiss the pernicious effects of that imperialism by defining it out of existence, as some might feel my generalized definition is intended to do. Rather, both because so much that is tendentious and doctrinaire has been written on the subject by the Canadian Left (which may readily be consulted by those who wish to foster the economics of resentment), and because I believe that we truly do not know enough yet about a great variety of economic questions — either in theory, or as matters of fact — I am more interested here in the "idea" of American imperialism as an operable truth in Canada's self-perception than I am in the objective data, much of which remains to be dug out. Further, I have just begun to grope towards the writing of a book on the nature of American imperialism as perceived in a comparative perspective, and I am both far too ignorant as yet of the fundamental data and too committed to arriving at no conclusions about the dynamics of American imperialism until those dynamics have been examined within a variety of contexts, rather than only one or two, to be prepared to abandon my present position of controlled (I hope) ambiguity.

Even so, however, and even given the fact that my concern here is with the intellectual perceptions of the idea of imperialism rather than with its economic dynamics, one cannot avoid the obligation of an interim report. This may best be expressed by suggesting that, despite certain reservations, I am much impressed by the kind of analysis recently put forward by R. T. Naylor of McGill University in his two-volume work, *The History of Canadian Business, 1867–1914*.[33] In an introductory statement, Eric Kierans asserts that, "There is not much difficulty in attempting to understand the structure of the Canadian corporate economy." I do not find this to be true at all; I think it quite difficult to understand, even though each corporation must file an annual return with the Minister of National Revenue. This has not always been so, and in any event I have a healthy scepticism for such returns, however audited, since I am disinclined to accept the notion that Canadian businessmen are *all* more honest than American businessmen (Seymour Martin Lipset said they were more conservative, and he said that Canadians as a group were more honest than Americans as a group, but he did not wed the two statements).[34] Naylor's book, fine as it is, also worries me because quite often, on subjects I do know quite a bit about, he falls into factual error, and at other times his style is so careless syntactically that one cannot be certain what he means. (The most worrisome example of this comes near the end of his second volume, when he may be suggesting that the growth of the British Empire had ceased by 1914, although he might also be suggesting that it continued well into the 1920s; whatever his point may be, the British Empire continued to grow into the 1930s.) Nor has Naylor's publisher served him well, although this is not to be held against the contents. Finally, it is all too evident that Naylor has written with a populist thesis in mind and that, while he does not tell us so, the moral fervour with which he condemns Canadian business for dishonesty and malfeasance suggests that he believes alternatives were possible and not chosen, alternatives which he fails to identify.

Having said this, however, I am still prepared to embrace Naylor's argument as my interim report. Let me summarize it briefly, and submit it to the same over-simplification to which I have submitted Messrs. Woodward, Potter, and Magdoff elsewhere. Let me also say at once that the reason Naylor's argument seems convincing to me is that he links it intelligently to the staple-dependency theories of Innis and Creighton, while revising them in significant ways; that he appears to be well aware of the staple-dependency theorists of Latin America (although he does not cite them) and has used them as I would wish them to be used, with a sense of comparative sophistication; and that his conclusion — one bound to lead the more avid Marxists to label him a bourgeois revisionist, a label I am happy to accept for myself even though Naylor appears to see himself as a radical — indicates that American imperialism was the product of Canadian responses to predictable American and British overtures, so that one must look to Canada, as I have already argued in other ways, if one is to understand American imperialism in Canada. Bay Street is at least as important as Wall Street (not a new thought), and the presence of Canadian collaborators, though a term not used to promote his analysis, is amply proved by Naylor.

Naylor is particularly concerned with the role of Canadian banks, although he does not neglect the transfer of technology, capital flows, the nature of foreign direct investment, or the tariff. He is interested in how capitalism worked, that is, how capital was accumulated and how this accumulation influenced the transition from commercial to industrial capitalism. Using dependency theory, Naylor sees capital as the means of satellitization of the periphery, and he examines Innis's "staple trap" — in which staple export within an imperial context obviously feeds the imperial rather than the domestic economy — in terms of American industrial power. Canadian banks, he concludes, were unwilling to finance Canadian secondary industry in the nineteenth century. They wished to finance the movement of Canadian resources onto world markets. By moving funds and capital generated in one region to another, they fostered further satellitization, and — in the case of the Atlantic provinces — underdevelopment. Such decisions (for *decisions* they were) meant that Canadian capitalism would be dependent on Americans in a variety of ways, of which he makes most of entrepreneurship, patents (here he supplies fascinating new research), branch plants, and direct investment.

Nor is Naylor inherently hostile to the bank as an institution, for he has some good things (and even slightly romantic and nostalgic things) to say about local banks in the Maritimes. Rather, his villains are the central banks. Increased centralization systematically choked off expansion of local industry, creating ever larger gaps between regions. The New York money market shaped Canadian industrialization. The result was a Canadian industry that was conservative, dependent on foreign capital and technology, and demanding of state assistance. "The greater success [*sic*] achieved in the introduction of American technology," he concludes, "the poorer the record of Canadian achievement."

While Naylor does not say so explicitly, he clearly finds the Galt tariff of 1859 less of a heroic document than others have felt it to be. This and subsequent tariffs encouraged trusts and were used as political weapons to re-establish reciprocal trade with the United States, a trade which — given the fact of dependence — could not be truly reciprocal in any meaningful sense of the word, and which simply meant that the National Policy would play into American hands. By restricting the growth of potential Canadian rivals to American corporations, the tariff as an instrument of policy strengthened the American subsidiaries operating in

Canada, nurturing multinational enterprises which were bound to be dominated from the United States.

There is more to it than this, of course. There were other options open to Canadian voters from time to time. The Canadian financial community could have made other choices. Some very real Canadian-based multinationals did arise. Other external capitalisms than the American did modify and compete with the continentally developing order of dependency. But the basic thrust of Naylor's analysis seems to me convincing, and its effect is double. It protects against Scylla and Charybdis: against that weakness of which Marc Bloch warned us, that there is nothing more dangerous than the temptation to take all things as natural, as not having involved conscious choices which might well have been different; and against the weakness of assuming that all fault lies external to oneself, that a rapacious American capitalism forced itself upon an innocent, struggling, and indefensible Canadian society.

The problem of perceiving the many complex phenomena which so frequently are grouped under the rubric of imperialism is not unlike the problem examined so intelligently by Sol Worth and John Adair in their book *Through Navajo Eyes*.[35] Worth was a film maker. He gave cameras to a number of Navajo who, he discovered, filmed quite different things, in quite different ways, than he would have done. They did not differ because of some alleged technological gap, for they were trained; they differed because, quite literally, what they saw in the world around them — what was important to them, what was "near" and what was "far", what linked together and what did not, what the finished film meant to say — was seen with different eyes. Such is the case with imperialism, and to force upon the word, or the complex phenomena, or the analysis of either, a single set of meanings is intellectually impossible (although no doubt politically expedient).

Canadians have sold themselves a bill of goods, to the

point that they often demean themselves. Consider two stories — one common, and one less common – that are virtually a part of Canadian folklore. The common story is that the Fathers of Confederation wished to name the new nation "the Kingdom of Canada", reflecting the monarchical principles upon which the state would be based. Anti-monarchical sentiment in the United States was strong, and anti-Canadian feeling was felt to be only slightly less strong. The legislature of the State of Maine expressed its concern, and rumour had it that Congress was exercised over the use of a name that might be viewed as an insult to the Monroe Doctrine. The Colonial Office and the Fathers of Confederation together chose another title, and, as we have seen, the key word "Dominion" was inserted into the BNA Act after Leonard Tilley, leader of the Liberal party in New Brunswick, plucked it out of Psalm 72, verse 8: "He shall have dominion also from sea to sea, and from the river unto the ends of the earth."[36] The hope was that the new nation — not in fact officially called a Dominion — would soon fulfil this prophecy, as, by 1873 it did. Whether "Dominion" was a weasel word, chosen because the Founding Fathers lacked the courage of their convictions about "Kingdom", or whether it was joyously chosen to reflect optimism about the future, the story that the term was virtually forced upon a reluctant nation from the need to placate unreasoning anti-monarchical protests from the United States was nevertheless well lodged in Canadian folklore. In any case, the manoeuvre, if it were such, did not work, for General Nathaniel Banks still rose on the floor of Congress to denounce the "Dominion" as contrary to the interests of the United States and a violation of the Monroe Doctrine. As Robin Mathews said in another context, "Canadians are colonised even in their liberation movements."

The less common story comes from 1919. In May of that year the Canadian House of Commons, no action being required by the Senate, voted to send to the King an address asking him "to refrain hereafter from conferring title of honour or titular distinction upon Canadians". So reported the press. The actual address was rather more florid although no less direct:

To the King's Most Excellent Majesty. Most Gracious Sovereign. We, Your Majesty's most dutiful and loyal subjects, the House of Commons of Canada in Parliament assembled, humbly approach Your Majesty, praying that Your Majesty may be graciously pleased: (a) To refrain hereafter from conferring any title of honour or titular distinction upon any of your subjects domiciled or ordinarily resident in Canada, save such appellations as are of a professional or vocational character or which appertain to an office. (b) To provide that appropriate action be taken by legislation or otherwise to ensure the extinction of an hereditary title of honour or titular distinction, and of a dignity or title as a peer of the realm, on the death of a person domiciled or ordinarily resident in Canada at present in enjoyment of an hereditary title of honour or titular distinction, or dignity or title as a peer of the realm, and that thereafter no such title of honour, titular distinction, or dignity or title as a peer of the realm, shall be accepted, enjoyed or used by any person or be recognized. All of which we humbly pray Your Majesty to take into your favourable and gracious consideration.[37]

This address was transmitted by the Governor General, the Duke of Devonshire, on June 12, and in due course it took effect. Today Prime Ministers of New Zealand or Australia may be knighted but Mr. Trudeau never shall be.

Soon we heard that Canadians eliminated the possibility of titles not only because such titles offended their democratic sensibilities but because they feared that Americans would view the continued use of them as yet one more piece of evidence that Canada was not an independent nation. It is true that in 1911 a bombastic American press and a number of silly Senators had talked again of annexation and that in 1919 there was strain between the United States and the United Kingdom. But it is also true that the key debate on the abolition of knighthoods for Canadians took place on May 22, while the Winnipeg General Strike had begun on

May 15, which is to say that the members of the Canadian House must have attached considerable importance to what they viewed, by a vote of ninety-four to forty-three, as a necessary democratizing step. It is also true that the British were irritated by the entire matter, for they felt that the King's answer should be that he "has no desire to exercise his prerogative of conferring honours . . . so long as the grant of such honours is not recommended by the Prime Minister of Canada." Given the address submitted to the King, the Canadian House should "rest assured that in these circumstances no honours will be granted in Canada". The whole affair "involves an absurdity", for the desired right could not be attained "unless Canada legislates to impose a penalty on e.g. Lord Beaverbrook's successor in the peerage if and when he shows his face in Canada".[38]

But the thing was done. The point here is that (despite the belief which grew in certain quarters later that the abolition of titles was but one more Canadian collapse in the face of an insensitive Republic) there is not a shred of evidence that the United States took a position on the matter, that Britain considered American sentiments in any way relevant, or that the Canadian legislators were looking across the border as they spoke or voted. Not a newspaper report, not a line of the debate, not a minuted despatch suggests that the episode was other than what it appeared to be: a political step to prove that Canada's leaders were, on such issues as these, "democrat to the hilt".

Myth dies hard. The United States is a convenient *deus ex machina*. If politicians can use the bogey of American annexationism to achieve their ends, so too can intellectuals. It is not only in golf that the bogey thrives. Barry Lord, writing in 1968, pointed to the idea of American imperialism as that which kept the people of Canada from realizing themselves: "We must take Canada back, *by whatever means our owner makes necessary* [my emphasis], and then give the resources and industries of this land to its own people. Let us organize a new Canada in which people, not American-controlled corporations, come first."[39] Sir Isaac Brock is dead but Sir Roger Hale Sheaffe lives. One must attack and attack again.

The study of Canadian history does help one understand the nature of American imperialism. Even more, it helps one grasp how Canadians perceive the idea that energizes the act. The study of American history no less, then, given the inextricable intertwining of the two histories, helps one to understand Canada. To assert the inseparability of the two historiographies is not to engage in some form of intellectual imperialism any more than it is to assert that one manifestly cannot understand French-Canadian separatism without English-Canadian history. To use comparative insights surely enriches the perspective on a single historiography. To know that areas which come late to industrialization tend to concentrate in cities and along transport lines, whether in the American West, in the developing countries, or in Canada as a whole, is to see a unity in which the genuinely unique stands out the more immediately. To see how Canada cannot be separated from the history of the British Empire, or from constituent parts of that imperial history, is not to diminish the Canadian sense of independence nor to aggrandize the Canadian contribution to the independence of others. To see that whatever form American imperialism may have taken in Canada has been altered substantially by myth, misunderstanding, and ideology is not to diminish the reality. And all such balances, such suggestions of cause and effect relationships, such comparisons, surely serve to show that Canadian history is exciting, widely relevant outside Canada's borders, and important to its citizens. As George Grant has wryly noted: "To think of the U.S is to think of ourselves — almost."[40] I have hoped to show that in important ways this is not so.

To be sure, to the conservative — which Grant is — or to the ironist, there is one incontrovertible similarity. Both national historiographies partake of the human condition. One wonders at the parochialism of a Margaret Atwood, who, in contrasting the imperialist United States with the perennial victim Canada, does not realize that there are neither victim nor executioners in the collective moral sense. That is, unless one accepts a truly dark vision of life. Cast in this manner, one can quickly learn that Americans see themselves as victims as well, although they nominate a more cosmic executioner. None expresses this universal vision of darkness better than that greatest of American writers, Herman Melville, in *Moby Dick*. In a chapter entitled "The Monkey Ropes", Melville shows how one human being is tied to another, literally, in that the harpoon man, away from the parent ship, is tied to a whaler aboard ship. Each must do his job both to protect the other and to save his own life. Shortly after making his point about mutual responsibility, Melville introduces his famous scene in which the little black boy, Pip, falls overboard and sinks to a great depth, pulled down by the White Whale; he loses consciousness, and, in a reverie and still alive by the merest fraction, is brought back by fortune and skill to the deck. In this moment of seeing death plain, Pip discovers that God goes ablackberrying amongst the worlds.

If this is a shared condition, so too is hope, a youthful expectancy, a desire to bring change, to unshackle oneself, to find the key to the shackles, to retain or recapture one's convictions that all may yet be made right with one's world. I conclude with Janet Adam Smith's final assessment of John Buchan, who as Lord Tweedsmuir played a significant part in Canadian history. Of himself he wrote that he disliked emotion not because he felt lightly but because he felt deeply. His biographer's words are worth thinking about when one contemplates the optimism that is said to be the hallmark of the New World:

It had been on the whole a fortunate life. Into his sixty-four years he had packed more activity than most men could expect in twice that span. He had left a shelf of books to entertain and a shelf to add to knowledge. He had played a number of parts with competence and success; his final rôle had been the most rewarding, and he had spent himself in it. He had been most happy in his marriage and his friends. He had not allowed his pain to sour his life, and he had not feared death. He had kept to the end his capacity for delight and his sense of expectancy. His boy's dreams were still bright.[41]

Frank Underhill, that lively Canadian historian, once wrote: "Canada's history is as dull as ditchwater and her politics is full of it."[42] Not so. Not a bit of it. The historian in any land and at any time has but three responsibilities. To be significant. To be interesting. To be true. Canadian history is, as I have tried to show, both significant and interesting. As for truth, we shall have to wait and see.[43]

REFERENCES

CANADIAN HISTORY AND THE CASE FOR COMPARATIVE STUDIES

Obviously the literature relating to comparative history, and to the various questions discussed here, is vast, and only the most immediate of references can be supplied.

1. Marc Bloch is often said to be the father of comparative history. A useful article is William Sewell, "Marc Bloch and the Logic of Comparative History", in *History and Theory*, VI, ii (1967), 208–18, and a valuable collection of essays which demonstrates the values and pitfalls of the comparative method is C. Vann Woodward, ed., *The Comparative Approach to American History* (New York: 1966). Units of comparison need not be defined geographically, as I have done here, for they also may be social systems. In essence, as Sewell notes, comparison is a method with particular relevance where explanatory hypotheses require testing.

2. The literature on Turner is extensive. A particularly good evaluation is by Howard R. Lamar in Marcus Cunliffe and Robin W. Winks, eds., *Pastmasters: Some Essays About American Historians* (New York: 1969).

3. David M. Potter, *People of Plenty: Economic Abundance and the American Character* (Chicago: 1954).

4. The following eight paragraphs are drawn in part from my own *The Myth of the American Frontier: Its Relevance to America, Canada and Australia* (Leicester: 1971), and my essay in Howard R. Lamar, ed., *The Reader's Encyclopedia of the American West* (New York: 1977).

5. C. Vann Woodward, "The Age of Reinterpretation", *American Historical Review*, LXVI (October 1960), 1–19. This is also the right moment to read Richard Slotkin,

Regeneration through Violence: The Mythology of the American Frontier, 1600-1860 (Middletown, Conn.: 1973).

6. In Hans Kohn, *The Idea of Nationalism: A Study of Its Origins and Background* (New York: Macmillan, 1944).

7. On the application of the Turnerian argument to Canada, see Michael S. Cross, *The Frontier Thesis and the Canadas: The Debate on the Impact of the Canadian Environment* (Toronto: 1970). Lord Curzon of Kedleston, in The Romanes Lecture for 1907, *Frontiers* (Oxford: 1907), has some suggestive things to say about the subject in the imperial context. I have found four recent titles of particular value: Carl Berger and Ramsay Cook, eds., *The West and the Nation: Essays in Honour of W.L. Morton* (Toronto: 1976), although like all *Festschriften* this is a mixed bag; Lewis G. Thomas, "The Umbrella and the Mosaic: The French–English Presence and the Settlement of the Canadian Prairie West", in John Alexander Carroll, ed., *Reflections of Western Historians* (Tucson: 1969); Lewis H. Thomas, ed., *Essays on Western History* (Edmonton: 1976); and Jorge Mañach, *Frontiers in the Americas: A Global Perspective* (New York: 1975). Barry M. Gough has written several excellent essays which show the ways in which British Columbia differed from the Canadian norm. See, in particular, "Keeping British Columbia British: The Law-and-Order Question on a Gold Mining Frontier", *The Huntington Library Quarterly*, XXXVIII (May 1975), 269–80. The next several paragraphs are drawn from my *Myth of the American Frontier*.

8. See Carl Berger, *The Writing of Canadian History* (Toronto: 1976), in which Canadian intellectual history comes of age.

9. This is in no way to dismiss the contributions of W. L. Morton, Morris Zaslow, J. H. Dales, J. M. S. Careless, and others, to various Canadian theses relating to North-

ernism, monarchy, Metropolitanism, and dependency theory.

10. I touch upon overlapping but rather different issues in "On Decolonization and Informal Empire", *American Historical Review*, LXXXI (June 1976), 540–56.

11. See H. J. M. Johnston, *British Emigration Policy, 1815–1830* (Oxford: 1972); and G.ıyneth Joy Parr, "The Home Children: British Juvenile Immigrants to Canada, 1868–1974", unpublished PhD dissertation (Yale University: 1977).

12. Here I draw briefly upon my own "Getting to Know the *Beau Sauvage*", in National Maritime Museum, Maritime Monographs and Reports, ii (1971), Greenwich.

13. J. R. Hale, *Renaissance Exploration* (London: 1968).

14. Philip Mason, *Patterns of Dominance* (Oxford: 1970).

15. The comparative literature is very thin. Colin M. Tatz, in an inaugural lecture, *Four Kinds of Dominion* (Armidale, N.S.W.: 1972), offers a view largely parallel to mine although arising from a different argument. On Australia, one may best begin with F. S. Stevens, ed., *Racism: The Australian Experience*, 3 vols. (Sydney: 1971–72). For Canada, one may well begin with E. Palmer Patterson, II, *The Canadian Indian: A History since 1500* (Toronto: 1972), and two provocative articles, Donald G. Baker, "Color, Culture and Power: Indian–White Relations in Canada and America", *The Canadian Review of American Studies*, III (Spring 1972), 3–20; and L. F. S. Upton, "The Extermination of the Beothucks of Newfoundland", *Canadian Historical Review*, LVIII (June 1977), 133–53.

16. This somewhat roseate view requires at least circumspect modification on the basis of Alan Ward, *A Show of Justice: Racial "Amalgamation" in Nineteenth Century New Zealand* (Toronto: 1973).

17. Quoted in Tatz, *Four Kinds of Dominion*, p. 11.

18. One must be careful of the press in Canada, it seems.

After I had given my three lectures, there appeared a flourish of newspaper reports in which it was said that I thought Canada was living in the nineteenth century. This is not what I said. The provisions in the federal Indian Act which were parallel to those of the British Columbia Evidence Act of 1894 were repealed in 1951. The federal act applied to criminal matters coming within Section 91 of the British North America Act, and the provincial act was applicable to most civil matters before the court. These provisions do not seem to have been challenged in the courts and were cited with approval by the British Columbia Court of Appeal in *Rex* v. *Antrobus* in 1947. For the original provincial act of 1894 see *Statutes of the Province of British Columbia . . . 1894* (Victoria), 57 Vic., 4th sess., 6th Parl., ch. 13, April 11.

19. Here I draw upon my own essay in Jane Fawcett, ed., *The Future of the Past: Attitudes to Conservation, 1147–1974* (London :1976). The essay is about what the British call "the associative boondoggle".

20. These not entirely random selections are drawn from personal visits. I am grateful to have discovered the pursuit of comparative historical sites, for it justifies travel almost anywhere.

21. "National Register of Historic Places: Annual Listing of Historic Properties", [U.S.] Department of the Interior, *Federal Register*, Part II (February 7, 1978).

22. National and Historic Parks Branch, Department of Indian Affairs and Northern Development, *National Historic Sites Policy* (Ottawa: 1968). For Ontario provincial plaques, see *Ontario Historic Sites, Museums and Plaques*, issued annually by the Ministry of Culture and Recreation.

23. See my *The Blacks in Canada* (New Haven: 1971).

24. With apologies to the many who have gone this way before.

THE IDEA OF THE MOTHER DOMINION

1. Ted Allbeury, *Snowball* (Philadelphia: 1974).
2. Karl Deutsch, *Nationalism and Social Communication: An Inquiry into the Foundations of Nationality* (Cambridge, Mass.: 1953), and *Political Community at the International Level* (Garden City, N.Y.: 1954). Also relevant here is Graham Spry, "Canada: Notes on Two Ideas of Nation in Confrontation", *Journal of Contemporary History*, VI, i (1971), 173–96.
3. The customary reference here is to John S. Galbraith, "The 'Turbulent Frontier' as a Factor in British Expansion", *Comparative Studies in Society and History*, II (January 1960), 150–68.
4. G. N. D. Evans, *Uncommon Obdurate: The Several Public Careers of J. F. W. DesBarres* (Salem, Mass.: 1969).
5. See James K. Chapman, *The Career of Arthur Hamilton Gordon, First Lord Stanmore, 1829–1912* (Toronto: 1964), and Deryck Scarr, *Fragments of Empire: A History of the Western Pacific High Commission, 1877–1914* (Canberra: 1968).
6. Anthony P. Haydon, *Sir Matthew Nathan: British Colonial Governor and Civil Servant* (Brisbane: 1976).
7. The following six paragraphs are drawn from the Jervois Papers, which are in my possession. I hope in time to publish a biography of Jervois, to which my entry on him for the *Australian Dictionary of Biography* (forthcoming) is a short preliminary statement.
8. This is a more complex point than it appears to be from the standard accounts: C. D. Cowan, *Nineteenth Century Malaya: The Origins of British Political Control* (London: 1961); C. Northcote Parkinson, *British Intervention in Malaya, 1867–1877 (Singapore: 1960);* and Emily Sadka, *The Protected Malay States, 1874–1895* (Kuala Lumpur: 1968).
9. See my *Canada and the United States: The Civil War Years* (Baltimore: 1960).

10. W. F. D. Jervois, *Report on the Defence of Canada and of the British Naval Stations in the Atlantic*, Part I on the Defence of Canada, February 1864, and a further report, *Together with Observations on the Defence of New Brunswick*, January 1865, as well as Part II of the first report, November 1864, all in my possession.

11. C. P. Stacey, *Canada and the British Army, 1846–1871*, rev. ed. (Toronto: 1963), p. 255.

12. Vincent Ponko, at California State College, Bakersfield, is attempting to initiate just such a study. Until then we do have Robert Heussler, *Yesterday's Rulers: The Making of the British Colonial Service* (Syracuse: 1963), and the continuing and fascinating work of A. H. M. Kirk–Greene (some of it unpublished), such as "The British Colonial Governor in the 20th Century: A Collective Profile", unpubl. paper (University of London, Institute of Commonwealth Studies: 1978). His bibliography/ summaries for *African Research and Documentation* are particularly valuable.

13. My calculations, based on lists of governors in David P. Henige, *Colonial Governors from the Fifteenth Century to the Present* (Madison: 1970).

14. John T. Saywell and John C. Ricker, *How Are We Governed?* (Toronto: 1961), p. 32. I have not seen the 5th edition, published in 1977.

15. The Saywell–Ricker list is in error on this point: 21 Vict., c. 2, Provincial, is the Cayley tariff of 1858; the Galt tariff was the following year (22 Vict., c. 2, Provincial).

16. *Sessional Papers*, XVIII (1860), Part 4, 4.

17. The standard authorities here are Donald C. Masters, *The Reciprocity Treaty of 1854* (London: 1937), and Orville John McDiarmid, *Commercial Policy in the Canadian Economy* (Cambridge, Mass.: 1946).

18. See H. V. Hodson, *The Great Divide: Britain–India–Pakistan* (London: 1969).

19. The 1931 and 1926 statements are conveniently juxta-

posed in Erwin Helms, ed., *The British Commonwealth: A Selection of Speeches and Documents* (Göttingen: 1960).

20. I elaborate briefly on this problem in "Die amerikanische Revolution als Quelle demokratischer Freiheiten", in Otto Molden, ed., *Zu den Grenzen der Freiheit* (Vienna: 1977).

21. Gerald M. Craig, *Lord Durham's Report* (Toronto: 1963), pp. i–xii. The following paragraph draws heavily on Craig's introduction to the Report.

22. George Bennett, ed., *The Concept of Empire: Burke to Attlee, 1774–1947*, 2nd ed. (London: 1962), p. 8.

23. Arthur Berriedale Keith, ed., *Speeches and Documents on British Colonial Policy, 1763–1917* (Oxford: 1961), pp. vii–viii.

24. R. MacGregor Dawson, *The Government of Canada*, 3rd ed. (Toronto: 1957), p. 14.

25. See my *Failed Federations: Decolonization and the British Empire*, Cust Foundation Lecture for 1970 (Nottingham: 1970).

26. *Hansard* (House of Lords), Nov. 19, 1947, p. 325.

27. John W. Cell, ed., *By Kenya Possessed: The Correspondence of Norman Leys and J. H. Oldham, 1918–1926* (Chicago: 1976).

28. Robert G. Gregory, "Crisis for the British Empire: The East African Challenge to the Durham Tradition", *The South Atlantic Quarterly*, LIX (Spring 1960), 147–62.

29. See especially Edward Grigg, *The Constitutional Problem in Kenya*, Cust Foundation Lecture for 1933 (Nottingham: 1933), p. 10. The Hilton Young Report, which refers to the Durham Report on page 87, officially was Cmd. 3234 (January 1929), *Report of the Commission on Closer Union of the Dependencies in Eastern and Central Africa*.

30. I think Gregory failed to see this point in his 1960 article, but he has corrected for it in his excellent book, *India*

and East Africa: A History of Race Relations within the British Empire, 1890–1939 (Oxford: 1971).

31. Lord Hailey, *An African Survey: A Study of Problems Arising in Africa South of the Sahara* (Oxford: 1938).

32. Ibid., p. 712.

33. "A Survey of Native Affairs in South West Africa", and "Confidential Report by Lord Hailey [on] Southern Rhodesia", both unpubl. mss., copies in my possession. I am grateful to the late Professor Arnold Toynbee of Chatham House and to Sir Frederick Pedlar for making copies of these two reports available to me. An original typescript is on deposit at Rhodes House, Oxford. Sir Frederick hopes to edit the one, and I the other, for eventual publication.

34. Ged Martin, *The Durham Report & British Policy: A Critical Essay* (Cambridge: 1972); and John Manning Ward, *Colonial Self-Government: The British Experience, 1759-1856* (Toronto: 1976). Martin is now in Ireland.

35. The analysis that follows is taken from R. MacGregor Dawson, *The Development of Dominion Status, 1900–1936* (Oxford: 1937); Philip G. Wigley, *Canada and the Transition to Commonwealth: British–Canadian Relations, 1917–1926* (Cambridge: 1977), which is particularly good; and especially from Sir Kenneth C. Wheare, *The Constitutional Structure of the Commonwealth* (Oxford: 1960), pp. 6–16.

36. Quoted in Wheare, *Constitutional Structure*, pp. 7–8.

37. See Max Beloff, *Imperial Sunset, I, Britain's Liberal Empire, 1897–1921* (London: 1969), p. 314, *et seq.*

38. See above, p. 47.

39. This argument is extended in my "On Decolonization and Informal Empire", *American Historical Review*, LXXXI (June 1976), 540–56.

40. The foregoing argument concerning a variety of constitutional points has been strengthened by five articles, all in the *Journal of Commonwealth Political Studies*, which

I cite together here to save space: David K. Fieldhouse, "Autochthonous Elements in the Evolution of Dominion Status: The Case of New Zealand", I (May 1962), 85–111; Robert I. Rotberg, "The Federation Movement in British East and Central Africa, 1889–1953", II (May 1964), 141–60; Ramsay Cook, "A Canadian Account of the 1926 Imperial Conference", III (March 1965), 50–63, which shows that the Canadian contribution was less than previously supposed; D. J. Heasman, "Canadian Preoccupations", V (March 1967), 19–37; and Angus Ross, "Reluctant Dominion or Dutiful Daughter? New Zealand and the Commonwealth in the Inter-War Years", X (March 1972), 28–44.

THE IDEA OF AMERICAN IMPERIALISM

When these lectures were delivered, it was suggested to me that the third lecture was "too allusive" and "too elliptical". Upon re-reading it, I agree with this criticism, but since I am at work on a book on precisely this subject, I have decided to let this chapter stand virtually as it was delivered.

1. See lectures I and II above.
2. Ronald Steel is an exception to this generalization.
3. See, for example, Hans-Ulrich Wehler, *Der Aufstieg des amerikanischen Imperialismus: Studien zur Entwicklung des Imperium Americanum, 1865–1900* (Göttingen: 1974).
4. *Encyclopaedia Americana*, 1972 International Edition, s.v. "colonialism" and "imperialism".
5. The reference here, of course, is to K. M. Panikkar, *Asia and Western Dominance: A Survey of the Vasco Da Gama Epoch of Asian History, 1498-1945*, new ed. (London: 1959).
6. See Bernard Porter, *The Lion's Share: A Short History of British Imperialism, 1850-1970* (London: 1975).

7. See my *Canadian-West Indian Union: A Forty-Year Minuet* (London: 1968).
8. See Robert Chodos, *The Caribbean Connection: The Double-Edged Canadian Presence in the West Indies* (Toronto: 1977).
9. This concept is explored in William Roger Louis, ed., *Imperialism: The Robinson and Gallagher Controversy* (New York: 1976).
10. Compare Norman C. Owen, ed., *Compadre Colonialism: Studies on the Philippines under American Rule*, Michigan Papers on South and Southeast Asia, no. 3 (Ann Arbor: 1971), and Yen P'ing Hao, *The Comprador in Nineteenth Century China: Bridge between East and West* (Cambridge, Mass.: 1970).
11. See especially Harry Magdoff, *Imperialism: From the Colonial Age to the Present* (New York: 1978).
12. Particularly Teresa Hayter in *Aid as Imperialism* (Harmondsworth, Middlesex: 1971).
13. See especially D. C. M. Platt, *Latin America and British Trade, 1806–1914* (London: 1972), and *Business Imperialism, 1840–1930: An Inquiry Based on British Experience in Latin America* (Oxford: 1978).
14. The phrase belongs to P. T. Bauer in "The Economics of Resentment: Colonialism and Underdevelopment", *Journal of Contemporary History*, IV (January 1969), 51–71.
15. James D. Cockcroft, André Gunder Frank, and Dale L. Johnson, *Dependence and Underdevelopment: Latin America's Political Economy* (New York: 1972); also, Frank's *Lumpen-Bourgeoisie: Lumpen-Development: Dependency, Class, and Politics in Latin America* (New York: 1972); and, especially, his *Capitalism and Underdevelopment in Latin America*, rev. ed. (New York: 1969). See also The Development Education Centre, Toronto, *Underdevelopment in Canada*, Canada File II (Toronto: c. 1975).

16. I refer to Lionel Tiger and Robin Fox's, *The Imperial Animal* (New York: 1971).

17. See especially "The Consumption of Dependency Theory in the United States", *Latin American Research Review*, XII, iii (1977), 7–24.

18. "Trends and Issues in Latin American Urban Research, 1965-1970", Part I, *Latin American Research Review*, VI, i (Spring 1971), 52, 54.

19. Richard Graham, *Britain and the Onset of Modernization in Brazil, 1850–1914* (Cambridge: 1968). See also Peter Winn, "British Informal Empire in Uruguay in the Nineteenth Century", *Past & Present*, no. 73 (November 1976), 100–126.

20. Margaret Atwood, *Survival: A Thematic Guide to Canadian Literature* (Toronto: 1972), and Bonnie Lyons, " 'Neither Victims nor Executioners' in Margaret Atwood's Fiction", *World Literature Written in English*, XVII, i (April 1978), 181–87.

21. Leo Johnston, Steve Moore, and Debi Wells, *Imperialism and the National Question in Canada* (Toronto: 1975), p. 5.

22. Robin Mathews and James Steele, eds., *The Struggle for Canadian Universities* (Toronto: 1969).

23. Richard Rose, ed., *Lessons from America: An Exploration* (New York: 1974).

24. See especially Hector Kinloch, "America, the Republic of Junk", in the proceedings of the 1976 Smithsonian conference, Allan Davis, ed., *America's Impact on the World* (forthcoming).

25. See C. W. E. Bigsby, ed., *Superculture: American Popular Culture and Europe* (London: 1975).

26. Daniel Bell, *The Cultural Contradictions of Capitalism* (New York: 1976).

27. Ernest Lee Tuveson, *Redeemer Nation: The Idea of America's Millennial Role* (Chicago: 1968).

28. Quoted in Norman Etherington, "Theories of Empire and Modern American Imperialism", *The Australian Journal of Politics and History*, xx (August 1974), 210–22.

29. William Roger Louis, *Imperialism at Bay: The United States and the Decolonization of the British Empire, 1941–1945* (New York: 1978). I wish to thank the author for allowing me to read the manuscript prior to publication.

30. I find the argument convincing in Owen T. Adikibi, "The Impact of U.S. Multinational Corporations in Africa: The Case of West Africa", pp. 181–229, in Robin W. Winks, ed., *Other Voices, Other Views: An International Collection of Essays from the Bicentennial* (Westport, Conn.: 1978), which I read in manuscript.

31. London Public Record Office (PRO), Colonial Office (CO) 42/948: code cablegram, July 7, 1911.

32. Recounted in Norman Lewis, *Naples '44* (London: 1977).

33. R. T. Naylor, *The History of Canadian Business, 1867–1914* (Toronto: 1975).

34. More than once, and especially in "Revolution and Counter-Revolution — The United States and Canada", in Thomas R. Ford, ed., *The Revolutionary Theme in Contemporary America* (Lexington, Ky.: 1965).

35. Sol Worth and John Adair, *Through Navajo Eyes: An Exploration in Film Communication* (Bloomington, Ind.: 1973).

36. For representative versions of the story see W. L. Morton, *The Kingdom of Canada: A General History from Earliest Times* (Toronto: 1963), p. 324; and J. M. S. Careless, *Canada: A Story of Challenge*, rev. ed. (Toronto: 1963), p. 248.

37. For the file on this subject, consult PRO, CO 42/1011: Gov. Gen. Devonshire 471, June 4th, 1919, with enclosures and 495, June 12th, 1919, also with enclosures.

38. Ibid., 495, p. [2].

39. " 'mericans", in Al Purdy, ed., *The New Romans: Candid Canadian Opinions of the U.S.* (Edmonton: 1968), p. 151.

40. In "From Roosevelt to LBJ", in ibid., p. 39. See also T. H. B. Symons, *To Know Ourselves: The Report of the Commission on Canadian Studies*, 2 vols. in one (Ottawa: 1975).

41. Janet Adam Smith, *John Buchan: A Biography* (London: 1965), p. 471.

42. See, finally, that rather gentle book, *The Star-Spangled Beaver* (Toronto: 1971), edited by John H. Redekop.

43. The absence of any statement about Quebec and the history of French Canada in the three chapters here leads me to remark on the obvious: to discuss Quebec in Canada seems to me at this time rather like carrying coals to Newcastle. Two comments seem in order, however. First, when I organize my Canadian history course for students at Yale I focus on three elements in Canadian studies: the comparison of Canada with the United States; the way in which Canada helped set precedents for the decolonization of empire; and the ways in which the relationship between English Canadians and French Canadians can be compared and contrasted with the relationship between whites and Afrikaaners in South Africa, examining the Afrikaaner and the French Canadian from the perspective of the "dual-fragment state" and the "garrison state". Second, if Paris was worth a mass, Canada is worth learning French for.